Philippines Call Centre Outsourcing

ROB O'MALLEY

CONTENTS

Introduction

The call centre outsourcing industry has had a profound impact on many aspects of The Philippines. Its growth has created wealth and employment but also a series of challenges. Since the turn of the millennium, an industry which barely existed now boasts half a million direct employees in addition to countless numbers of indirect jobs. Its growth has swept aside all before it including the once dominant Indian industry. This book examines the industry in detail from its inception to its future from an industry expert who has seen first-hand how the industry has developed in a country whose economic prosperity had been written off. It will explain the highly complex and diverse nature of the industry which exists today along with the challenges it will need to address if it truly to achieve its potential of changing a nation. This book lays out impartial information based on facts, experience and countless conversations on the topic. Its aim is to highlight the real truth about the industry including the good, the bad and the ugly.

There have been many articles written on the call centre industry in The Philippines but I felt that the majority of this was simply marketing material trying to promote the country, a particular company or a specific service offering. I therefore felt compelled to write this book as an independent version of the industry highlighting both its positive aspects but also the challenges which have been addressed and those which remain. In my extensive experience in The Philippines call centre industry, I have discovered that there are a large number of commonalities between those companies and ideas which produce a positive outcome and those which produce a negative one. By highlighting these commonalities, I believe this book can provide useful insight for people working for vendors of outsourcing companies and their clients. I remain very positive about the potential of The Philippines as a call centre destination but I firmly believe that there are many instances where both vendors and clients can do things better. I have lived and breathed the industry for the past 13 years and I truly hope my experiences can assist you in your endeavours. If you ever wish to contact me to discuss anything related to the industry, you are more than welcome to do so. My email address is rob.omalley@call-centres.com and my phone number is +44 77400 96598. I look forward to speaking with you.

Chapter 1

How the industry developed

"From zero to national hero in 13 years, call centres continue to be the nations' sunshine industry".

In 2000, the economy of The Philippines was in a dire situation. Its neighbours seemed to have recovered from the 1997 Asian Financial Crisis but in Manila and elsewhere in the archipelago, there was a very different story. Even in the new business district of Ortigas, half-completed buildings littered the skyline & in Makati, some of the nation's finest office real estate remained unoccupied. Unemployment was still high and the country was highly dependent on the remittances of the millions of Filipinos who worked across the more prosperous nations of Asia, Europe, The Middle East and North America. Counties in the region such as Thailand, Malaysia and Singapore had started to grow their economies and had a renewed sense of optimism about their future prosperity. China was emerging as a global manufacturing powerhouse and India's outsourcing boom had already started to improve its own nation's economy. In sharp contrast, The Philippines was still searching for its place in an increasingly globalised world. The country's economy did have some bright spots most notably its semi-conductor industry but this alone was not going to provide for the ever-increasing number of young Philippine talent. Many Government officials were enviously admiring the growing outsourcing in India especially its English-speaking call centre sector. After all, The Philippines has always had much higher levels of English proficiency than India and a service culture which had proved rich pickings for many of the world's leading international hotel chains and airlines.

The exact date that the international call centre outsourcing industry started in The Philippines is a subject of much debate. Prior to 2000, there was a small local call centre industry servicing the domestic market and there were a handful of centres servicing the wider East Asian region. One of these was a company called McQueen International based out of Scotland who in 1997 had been purchased by Sykes. Whilst it was small in terms of the numbers of agents it employed in Manila, they provided Asian-language support to a number of companies predominantly in the technology sector. However, The Philippines has only ever had a very limited supply of Asian-language speakers and for the call centre industry to grow, the country had to look at her former colonial power of The United States. The history of the American presence in The Philippines meant that English was widely spoken in many areas of Philippine society from business to Government and the two countries shared a number of cultural similarities.

Most of the call centre world was looking at India but there were already a small number of companies already started to service The US market from The Philippines. At this time, the industry was mainly focused in Metro Manila and a much smaller number in the area of the former US Air Force base in Clark In the province of Pampanga. AOL had established a web chat centre in Clark and close by was the newly formed Cyber City Teleservices. In Metro Manila itself, the centres were focused around 3 locations; Makati City, Ortigas (part of Pasig) and Eastwood (part of Quezon City).

The centres which existed at the time predominantly consisted of 3 types of vendor; (1) Companies such as People Support who had raised investment capital to open their facility (2) Locally-owned conglomerates which had branched out into call centre operations often using their own businesses as incumbent clients (3) Local entrepreneurs such as Globastride with small centres ranging from 10-200 seats of capacity. Some of the latter group had also tied up with American entrepreneurs who would be the source of their new business from overseas. Importantly, very few of the international operators were in The Philippines and even the exceptions to this rule were not operating as offshore outsourcers as we know them today. Sykes were still very much focused on the domestic and regional markets and Teleperformance had a partnership with a local investor who predominantly provided domestic support services. All of these were in sharp contrast to the Indian market where not only had the international outsourcers already set up sizeable operations but many foreign companies were also establishing their own captive facilities. The Philippine Government clearly wanted to replicate the Indian model but an impeachment trial of the then President, Joseph Estrada, was shifting focus from improving the economy and also detracting many foreign investors.

On January 20th 2001, I turned on the television in my Manila hotel room to discover that a popular uprising was taking place less than 2 miles away. Among the small group of us who were in The Philippines to grow the call centre industry, I'm sure I wasn't the only one who had my bags packed ready to fly home but my concerns were ill-founded. After a peaceful day of protest, Estrada was no longer President and The Vice President, Gloria Arroyo had taken over power. Some might think that it's a coincidence but it's hard to ignore the fact that the next 24 months saw a dramatic upturn in the fortunes of the industry. The new Presidential administration placed a much greater emphasis on the inward investment authorities in attracting new entrants to the market. Arroyo herself was a Masters Graduate in Economics and it was no surprise that she made fixing The Philippines economy as a top priority. The Philippines was now set to woo foreign investors and Mar Roxas was the man who would champion the international market effort. Like Arroyo, Roxas was part of a political dynasty and like Arroyo, he was also an economist. In his role as Secretary of the Department of Trade & Industry, a huge emphasis was placed on working with industry experts to create an environment which would attract foreign investors. With such a competent individual as Roxas at the helm, The Philippines was well-positioned to market itself to foreign call centre companies. By the time Roxas, resigned his post in December 2003 to run as a candidate for The Philippine Senate, The Philippines was already a major player in the call centre market.

Whilst the growth in the number of call centre agents employed in the industry has been fairly constant, this period of 2001 to 2004 saw a rapid rise in the number of international outsourcing vendors mainly from The United States but also from Europe entering The Philippines marketplace for the first time. The Philippines Board of Investments ploughed a large proportion of their limited resources into encouraging outsourcing companies to set up in the country. There was growing concern in The United States regarding customer dissatisfaction with Indian call centres and this was the first time the phrase "Anywhere But India" was used by companies buying outsourced services. The American companies came to The Philippines in the droves and the vendors who were already there such as People Support & ETelecare went through a period of rapid expansion.

The Improving Image

In 2001, Asian Call Centres produced a report entitled "The Asian Call Center League Tables" which ranked the countries of Asia for their suitability for English speaking call centres. The Philippines ranked 1st overall pushing India into 2nd place. The report was widely reproduced in various magazines and was also used by Philippine Government officials in promoting themselves overseas. This was the first time that any research had questioned the dominance of India in this marketplace. The major analysts firms were still indicating that the India would remain the industry leader but they were now being slightly more bullish on their opinions of The Philippines.

A report was produced by Hong Kong based Political and Economic Risk Consultancy (PERC), which stated The Philippines was "the only Southeast Asian nation besides Singapore with a labour force with the potential to move beyond a manufacturing focus to a higher value-added level". PERC ranked the Philippines as fourth in Asia on quality of labor force, behind more expensive locations such as Japan, Taiwan, and Singapore. Across the world, the image of The Philippines as an offshoring destination was on the rise. The Philippine peso was also weak at around 50 pesos to the dollar although it had improved slightly from the height of the Estrada impeachment trial. This fact along with growing wage inflation in India made The Philippines an increasingly viable option.

Multi-Shoring

One thing which was The Philippines call centre industry could not have foreseen was military stand-off between India and Pakistan in May of 2002. The stand-off saw India expel the Pakistani Ambassador and Indian Prime Minister Vajpayee warned his troops to prepare for a decisive battle. Many call centre clients had grown rapidly in India but there was now a train of thought that they should de-risk by outsourcing work to multiple locations in case war broke out on the sub-continent.

A number of Indian vendors that I spoke with at the time claimed that they lost out on some major deals specifically because of the military stand-off with almost every single account going to companies in The Philippines instead. Even more importantly than a few new client wins for The Philippines, this incident changed the way in which many global companies now viewed sourcing for call centre vendors. Companies could no longer risk having all of their call centres in one country otherwise they run the risk of exposure in case of war or natural disaster. Instead, many would choose to de-risk by spreading their call centres over different countries and The Philippines was the obvious beneficiary of this change in thought process. Although clients weren't removing business from India, they were looking to other countries to outsource additional work. This is known as multi-shoring and for the first time on any significant scale, it enabled clients to determine which country was best able to meet their key performance indicators. In many of these cases, The Philippines outperformed India in areas such as customer satisfaction and language capabilities. The Philippines had now proven that it could compete and even out-perform its Indian rivals and this proved to be pivotal in determining the success of the call centre industry in The Philippines.

In 2002, I wrote an article for a magazine entitled "The Future of Offshore Call Centres". I made a number of predictions but there was 1 which prompted over 50 emails. I suggested that The Philippines would one day take over from India as having the most offshore call centre agents. All of the replies I had disputed my claim including one person who described the idea as "bonkers"! Even a Filipino who is very prominent in the industry told me that they'd "be happy to be number 2". However, I was not alone in my bullish assessment of the future of The Philippine industry. In the 12 months which followed, there was a massive influx of potential clients and new vendors visiting Manila. One of these was a man from a major financial institution who I'd agreed to meet in the lobby at The Shangri-La in Makati. He came down from his room and the first words he said to me were "I've already decided to outsource all our call centre activity here". Like many of the visitors at that time, his round-the-world trip had taken him to various cities in India before arriving in Manila and he'd made his rather quick decision based on the fact that his driver from the airport along with all of the hotel staff were incredibly polite and all spoke perfect English. This was his first ever visit to The Philippines and he'd been knocked back by the way he felt so at home in Makati. I informed him that if he was impressed by the standard of English he'd met so far, he would be expecting a real treat when we finally got to see some call centre agents later that evening. Although not every company I met at that time made decisions so rapidly, I can't think of 1 company I met at that time who visited both India and The Philippines and subsequently chose India as their preferred destination. Within The Philippines itself, the term "sunshine industry" was now being widely used to describe the industry. The country had finally found an industry where it could compete on the world stage and the best was yet to come.

Everything was coming together to create the perfect situation for The Philippines call centre industry; concerns over India, increased competitiveness, political stability and a shift towards multi-shoring were all starting to make The Philippines a very feasible option. However, the thing which made The Philippines even more ideal for foreign investors was the Government incentives. Companies could get incentives such as extended income tax holidays along with a whole load of other support and incentives. India simply couldn't compete and the growth in The Philippines accelerated at an even faster rate. Far from being a second-choice to India, The Philippines was fast becoming the preferred option.

2003 saw another highly significant milestone for the call centre industry. Industry leaders were concerned that the use of Philippine languages in the education system would prevent the expansion of the call centre industry. Based in part on lobbying from the industry, President Arroyo instructed the Department of Education to restore English as the medium of instruction in schools and universities. Not only did this send out the message to the call centre industry that The Philippines was ready for business but has also ensured a greater supply of suitable labour in the long-term.

From 2004, the industry grew at over 50% for several years and in terms of new accounts being won, The Philippines was already on a par with India by 2005. The Philippines was catching up with India and the reason that India had more call centre agents was because the Indian vendors had signed huge numbers of multi-year contracts with clients. When these contracts came up for renewal, many of them would move to The Philippines sometimes even with the same vendor they had worked with in India.

2004 saw the creation of The Business Process Association of The Philippines (BPAP). A number of initiatives at creating an industry-wide body had been tried before but this group had the backing of all major parties and senior Government officials. 2004 also saw Indian-based Hinduja buy C-Cubed and SOCA in The Philippines. Investors and Philippine based entrepreneurs were increasingly taking notice of the industry and People Support listed on The NASDAQ in the same year. Between 2004 & 2006, many of the large, long-term deals which had been signed in India were coming to an end and client dissatisfaction with many vendors in India led many clients to look outside of India instead of extending those relationships. Some clients decided to take call centre jobs back to The United States but many more chose to move their operations to The Philippines.

By 2007, we had started to see the first companies with in excess of 10,000 agents in The Philippines. One very interesting aspect of this was that a number of the larger companies had started off purely as Philippines based operations but had either been acquired by larger organisations or had set up facilities in other geographies. These included ETelecare (now part of Stream), People Support (now part of Aegis) and Ambergris Solutions (now part of Telus). This period saw continued expansion and there were more Indian vendors purchasing Philippines based operations. One of the smaller deals involved Chennai-based Allsec Technologies purchasing Kingdom Builders in Manila. By 2007 the industry had become so important that The Government decided to tap consulting firm McKinsey to produce a roadmap for the industry to provide guidance on how to expand whilst avoiding the mistakes made in India.

After 50% growth for the Philippines call centre industry in 2007, The Philippines was about to be dealt a blow to its expansion in the form of the Financial Crisis which swept America and very soon after, The UK and the rest of Europe. The financial services industry is the biggest single outsourcer of call centre jobs to The Philippines and people within the industry knew that the slowdown in the sector would be bad news. Companies such as Washington Mutual (WaMu) and others were significant outsourcers to The Philippines and their demise hit a number of vendors hard. At the time, there were also concerns whether the resulting economic downturn would have an impact on outsourcing from other sectors. A number of retailers were suffering from a downturn and they were faced with the decision as to whether to focus on their dwindling domestic centres or on cost cutting measures and offshore the work to cheaper destinations such as The Philippines. In the end, different companies took different approaches with some keeping work at home and others ramping up their offshore operations. The economic uncertainty and the lack of access to capital meant that outsourcing to both onshore and offshore locations was actually increasing as companies opted against building their own captive operations. Some companies even chose to sell of their US-based captive operations and cash-rich offshore outsourcing companies snapped them up at bargain prices with the hope of offshoring some of the roles and to be able to offer a blended onshore/offshore solution. One example of this was Aegis who bought the facilities of Sallie Mae in Texas and ended up offshoring some of the roles to The Philippines. One other sector which took a significant hit was the travel sector where companies such as Expedia had been long-time advocates of The Philippines for their outsourcing requirements. The economic downturn meant that 2009 was a comparatively slow time but it is a testament to the popularity of Philippine call centres that they grew at all and at a faster rate than its Indian rivals.

By 2010 the industry rebounded and for the first time, The Philippines had overtaken India as the largest offshore call centre destination and this was met with glee across the nation. On a personal level, I was glad that I could no longer be considered "bonkers" for predicting this back in 2002. Growth in The Philippines remains higher than in India but there are many who believe that the ever increasing demand for call centre agents is not sustainable without increasing the volume of work conducted outside of Metro Manila.

The Industry Today

By 2013, The Philippines call centre industry had grown to a level beyond even the wildest dreams of those who championed it in during the early stages. Sub-industries supporting call centres and their workers have flourished and the industry now brings in billions of dollars to the country every year. The country itself has a renewed sense of optimism and this is in no small part to outsourcing and offshoring especially of call centres. The industry now represents a very significant portion of the total Philippine economy even without taking into consideration its indirect impact.

It's hard to think of The Philippines without its call centre industry. Where would these half a million young Filipinos be working now? Would they have emigrated or would the country have continued with its economic demise?

Many companies now view The Philippines as integral part of the call centre offering but equally, there are many companies who for whatever reason have decided that they don't wish to offshore their call centres at all or choose the alternatives to The Philippines. This includes some of the world's largest outsourcers of call centre activity such as Vodafone who have multiple offshore locations but have specifically opted not to outsource to The Philippines. There are also a number of companies have tried and failed to make The Philippines work for their call centre operations. Although there are comparatively few of these, when a client fails in an offshore location, they typically choose to move that work to another location rather than choose another vendor in the same country. The Philippines was the beneficiary of many such instances from India. Both internal and external challenges remain to build on the success of the past 13 years and these are discussed throughout this book.

Chapter 2

Recruitment & Retention

"According to a report by The Philippine National Statistics Office in May 2013, 18% of the country's unemployed are college graduates. White collar employment is high in the country which makes many question why recruitment is such a hot topic but it is".

There is one very good reason why I've included the topic of recruitment and retention so early on in book and that's because it's such a substantial issue. The challenge of recruiting and retaining enough quality staff is undoubtedly the biggest obstacle facing all vendors but The Filipinos are highly creative and have applied this to ever more inventive staff attraction strategies. As someone who regularly assesses Philippine based call centres for my clients, I can tell you that there is rarely a more important factor than a vendor's ability to attract and retain quality staff in sufficient. This isn't something which is unique to The Philippines but the nature of the competition for staff in Manila makes this absolutely crucial.

To industry outsiders, the issue of recruitment might appear bizarre. The country has a population of over 100 million people including one of the youngest and fastest growing populations in the world. With over 400,000 graduates produced annually and with good English being spoken by most of them, it may seem strange that recruitment is an issue at all.

Things weren't always this challenging. Back in 2001, I needed to recruit 10 agents for a pilot campaign for a British company. I decided that we should adopt a very common approach and take out a relatively small advert in the Sunday edition of The Manila Bulletin in order to promote a recruitment open day. The open day attracted over 1,000 candidates and we literally had people queuing down the street waiting to get in. The quality of the applicants was incredibly high and needless to say that the pilot was a huge success. We could have easily recruited over 100 of these applicants but we simply cherry-picked the best 10 who I would have recruited in any call centre anywhere in the world. Our call centre grew throughout 2001 and 2002 and we continued to attract exceptional candidates. In 2002, we were offered a very large campaign and I spoke with our HR Manager to ascertain our strategy for the recruitment and what I learnt in that meeting shocked me. In the previous months, we hadn't done any advertising for staff. One of the HR team had printed a large volume of leaflets about our call centre and every Sunday had bought the Manila Bulletin to work out which call centres were having open days. Then, she would go the location of the open days and give the leaflets to people at the backs of the queues. My initial reaction was one of shock. I wouldn't want my competitors piggy-backing on the back of my recruitment campaigns and felt we should offer the same respect to others. I put an end to this practice but you can't deny that the HR assistant had shown a great deal of initiative and initiative would be something very much needed by recruitment teams as the industry progressed. This also highlighted the over-supply of suitable talent which existed back in 2001-2002. Fast forward to today and this supply is more than met by the massive demand for agents.

Changing Practices

In the early days, the high-end call centres would generally only employ graduates from the top universities in the country such as Ateneo, De La Salle and University of The Philippines. As the industry expanded, these universities could no longer provide enough graduates and so call centres increasingly recruited from a wider range of universities. Some call centres even felt that the graduates from the top universities were actually not as suitable as other universities as their graduates were often more interested in other careers. Some call centres have now even started recruiting from people who had not graduated. Of course, in Western countries, only a small percentage of graduates work in call centres although their numbers have increased due to the economic downturn. However, in The Philippines, it's still widely regarded that applicants must have at least some tertiary education to have the skills needed for all positions from call centre agent upwards.

In 2013, the demand for call centre agents outstrips supply. Estimates suggests that The Philippines produces 400,000 graduates annually from tertiary institutions and every year, the demand for call centre agents is growing by 100,000 per year. However, not every graduate wants to work night shifts in a call centre and so the industry has to be highly creative in sourcing candidates from other industries and establishing other sources of talent.

The acceptance rates among call centre applicants have always been fairly low. It's estimated that only 3-5% of applicants are successful with higher percentages recorded by lower-tiered suppliers such as those focused on low-end telemarketing activity. There have been various initiatives to increase the acceptance rate. For example, some centres refer those candidates who narrowly fail their tough English-proficiency tests to training centres. These training centres are then either paid by the candidate to undergo training or paid a placement fee by the call centre if their improved skills enable them to pass a reassessment. Purely anecdotal evidence suggests that several thousand people have found employment in this way. This may seem a small amount compared to the vast size of the industry but with supply outpaced by demand, every initiative helps. Many of those who fail the assessments also found more success when applying to the lower-tiered vendors who will typically pay lower salaries. After spending several months speaking with Americans or other English speakers 8 hours a day, their skills are often to a level where they can reapply to the higher-tiered operations and are often successful.

Increasing The Labour Supply

With such strong demand for agents, Government and industry officials have been keen to look at specific approaches to increase the labour pool. The BPAP Roadmap provides for a number of specific initiatives aimed at achieving this such as the following:

(1) Tapping alternative labour pools. In Western countries, many call centres employ large number of housewives to assist with peak call centre traffic. This is rare in The Philippines but some call centres are now proactively targeting this group.

(2) Employing students to work to finance their studies. In The Philippines, it is rare for students to work part-time during their studies and instead rely on their families for financial support. The outsourcing industry hopes to change this.

(3) Expand the number of call centres outside of Metro Manila so that those who want to remain in their province can still do so.

(4) Work with the education sector to make curricula more beneficial to students seeking a career in the industry. To an extent, this is happening already

The Inventive Attraction Strategies

With such strong demand for call centre agents, outsourced vendors have had to become increasingly innovative with their attraction strategies and here are some of the strategies used:

- The use of online recruitment database and job posting sites are commonplace within the majority of outsourcing companies. These include jobstreet.com, jobsdb.com and phil-job.com.
- The Philippines is widely regarding as one of the text messaging capitals of the world. The highly social nature of the Filipino people together with the low cost of sending such messages in the country makes text messaging (SMS) very popular with over 2 billion text messages sent every year. Marketers of all products use text messaging very actively in The Philippines and many call centres use this promotional facility to search for new candidates. A number of different services exist to target potential candidates and the results have been mixed.
- Job fairs are also common-place in The Philippines and it would be rare to see one where call centre companies were not represented. There have even been call centre specific job fairs which have attracted thousands of potential candidates. In many graduate recruitment fairs, more than 50% of exhibitors have been call centre companies.
- Leaflet distribution within areas of high footfall such as in shopping malls and close to sporting events is also one strategy deployed. Some companies have even used leaflet distribution outside universities towards the end of the academic year.
- The newspaper industry used to be the prime source for new candidates and whilst their use for call centre recruitment campaigns is still widespread, their share of the total recruitment advertising marketplace has diminished as

vendors have been forced to use ever more dynamic attraction campaigns to meet the growing demand for personnel.

- Prior to the start of the offshoring boom, most Filipino recruitment agencies were focussed on the provision of staff for positions in other countries in areas such as domestic workers and nurses. There were a few recruitment companies focussed on domestic recruitment which were a run by either local entrepreneurs or franchise style arrangements with the global recruitment agencies. Since the call centre industry took off, these recruitment agencies have moved into the supply of call centre personnel and a number of call centre focused agencies have sprung up specifically to provide all levels of call centre employees.
- Signing on bonuses are not uncommon within some vendors. I've heard of some companies paying as much as 40,000 pesos (about USD1,000 or GBP650) just for an agent to take a role. Such high amounts are rare but the use of more moderate signing bonuses are increasing in their popularity. Relatively large signing on bonuses are almost unheard of in markets such as The United States, The United Kingdom or Australia.
- Employee-get-employee bonus schemes are also fairly common with outsourced vendors paying existing staff to refer their friends and family for work. This has been a highly successful strategy for many vendors. The employee who sources their friend is given an amount as a bonus which is normally slightly less than would be paid to an external recruitment agency and is paid after training is complete or after a fixed period of service. One downfall to this has been that friends often tend to leave together to go to their next job.
- The now defunct outsourced vendor Epixtar used some of the hosts from MTV Philippines in their banner advertising and used them on huge billboards on the main routes into areas which were saturated with call centres. There is an increase of all types of banners and billboards along busy highways.

- Some centres have even set up retail-style recruitment and assessment centres in areas such as the country's many shopping malls. Candidates can enter these centres where they can discuss the available roles and even conduct initial assessment screenings to assess their suitability.

Recruitment Process

The recruitment process in The Philippines is very similar to that adopted in the Indian industry and would typically include far more processes than would be required in an onshore contact centre.

Processes vary from operation to operation but a typical recruitment process would go something like this:

- Manpower Requisition – The Operations Department will tell the HR process the specifications of staff requirements including volumes, start dates and required skill sets.
- Sourcing – The HR team will go through the sourcing process using some of the methodologies described earlier in this chapter.
- Initial Phone Interview – The HR personnel will conduct a basic interview over the telephone in order to short-list candidates
- Testing – Those that pass the initial telephone screening will go on to take tests normally within the vendor's location.
- Language Assessment – This will be a detailed assessment of the candidates English-language skills. This is highly thorough and will screen out a large percentage of the candidates.
- Behavioural Interview – Many call centres believe the candidate attitude for a role in call centres is on a par with the requirement for language skills. The behavioural interview will assess the candidates suitability for the role
- Operations Interview – The people who would be managing the candidate after employment then conduct their own interview.

- Background Check – This includes reference checking and seeking NBI (National Bureau of Investigation) Clearance. NBI clearance is a Government run scheme to guarantee that the candidate does not have any criminal convictions.
- Pre-Employment Medical Exam. There are concerns that night shift work can have a detrimental impact on someone's health especially for people with pre-existing conditions and so this examination ensures they are in good health.
- Job Offer. This is formally documented
- Induction Training. This normally takes place in the same time zones as the agent will be working to get them used to the shift
- New Employee Orientation

Team Leaders & Middle Management

Most companies try to recruit as many team-leaders from within their existing employees but during high periods of growth, the percentage of external recruits for these positions will often increase.

In the early stages of the call centre boom, there was a disproportionately large number of expats in management and training positions based in The Philippines. Given that these are relatively expensive resources, the percentage of Americans compared with the total workforce has dropped sharply. There is still a sizeable American presence in the call centre industry in addition to people from other countries such as The UK and Australia. Work-permits for these individuals are quite easy to obtain but should be done with professional legal assistance. The Government has made work permits for foreigners in the outsourcing industry easier to obtain as part of their incentive schemes to attract outsourcing companies. Many of the expats in the industry are people who were already living in The Philippines due to marital commitments but have been lured by the call centre industry in the absence of other available careers. These individuals tend to command lower salaries than those brought specifically to the country by the vendors.

In almost every Indian owned call centre vendor in The Philippines, the country manager will be Indian and in many of these companies, there will be large numbers of Indians either permanently based in The Philippines or during periods of expansion. The slowdown in the Indian call centre industry has meant that there are large numbers of Indians with extensive management experience which has been very useful to the industry.

The vast majority of the expats enjoy The Philippines and this is no surprise as in a quality of life survey conducted by HSBC (2011), the Philippines ranked eighth globally.

Attrition

Attrition is a major issue for the call centre industry in The Philippines despite efforts from some to suggest that it isn't. The way in which attrition is calculated and even misreported by many vendors makes the comparison between different countries an impossible task. However, anecdotal evidence suggests that attrition rates are slightly lower than India but still very high. Industry figures suggest that attrition rates are 35-40% in outsourcing firms and less in captive centres. From all of the evidence I have collated, these figures are underestimated. The fact that attrition is lower in captive centres represents a number of factors such as slightly higher salaries, more structured career paths and the kudos many Filipinos feel when working for well-known international brands. More importantly, attrition is higher in Philippine call centres that their equivalents in The United States. There is little factual evidence to suggest that any there is significant difference between the vendors when comparing on a like-for-like basis. High attrition clearly comes with high costs and potential quality issues and some clients have expressed concerns at alarmingly high attrition rates.

The most interesting aspect of attrition is that most of the people leaving one call centre are simply going to another call centre as opposed to leaving the industry all together. It's not unusual for someone to leave a job to go and work for another vendor in the same building. One way that a number of vendors have tried to stem the flow of attrition to other centres is through the use of bi-lateral and multi-lateral non-compete agreements. This effectively means that centres will not accept applicants who currently work for one of the other parties to the non-compete agreement. Sometimes, these agreements also disqualify agents who have worked for another party to the agreement within a fixed time-frame after finishing with one of the vendors. The main challenge to these agreements has been that new entrants to the market have been very aggressive in the labour market and refuse to sign up to such agreements & they simply poach staff from other centres. After establishing themselves in the market, they discover the pains of inter-industry competition and then often want to become part of these agreements.

As we saw in India, the attrition rate to alternative vendors will normally go down when the growth rate reduces and I fully expect this to happen in The Philippines. However, attrition to roles outside the industry often increases when the growth rate slows down as the opportunities for rapid career advancement within the company and the wider industry are diminished.

Overall, The Philippines needs to continue its development of its educational changes to improve the availability of English-speaking agents with critical thinking skills. There also needs to be further development for providing sufficient numbers of people who have the potential to move into middle and senior management roles. There is also scope to improve the numbers of people who have the required skills to set up and manage the various call centre technologies. At present, many of the Indian owned outsourcing companies manage much of their technology infrastructure from India or bring in qualified personnel from India to work in these roles.

Chapter 3

Accent, Language & Communication Style

"The Philippines prides itself on being the 3rd largest English speaking nation in the world but for most Filipinos, English is their 2nd language and there are differences in the way in which Filipinos communicate compared to the Westerners they service in call centres"

One of the main reasons given for call centres moving from India to The Philippines was consumer dissatisfaction with the accent of the Indian call centre agents together with poor communication skills in English. It's often said that the Filipinos speak English with a neutral American accent. Whilst this isn't technically true, it's generally accepted that the typical Filipino agent is easier for an American to understand a Filipino accent than their Indian equivalent. However, a client of mine outsources a large amount of call centre traffic to The Philippines and conducted 1000s of post-call surveys with the people who had called their call centre. The overwhelming issue raised was that of the inability to understand their English and their accent. There are plenty of other companies who have conducted similar surveys which have often produced similar results. Therefore, to say that accent and language is not a potential issue is a mistake. In this chapter, I will examine some of the common languages issues associated with Philippine call centres and provide some advice on what successful call centres have done to overcome them.

Style of Communication

Filipinos typically have a far more relaxed communication style compared with their equivalents in Western countries and there are concerns that this is responsible for increased Average Handle Time (AHT) than would be experienced in a domestic centre. This is not only expensive but it is frustrating for the end customer who will often become irate if the agents take too long to get to resolve their issue. Estimates for the amount of additional time a Filipino will take vary between 5 and 50%.

The metric of average handle time has been eliminated from many call centre operations as it is widely believed that it forces agents to communicate in a different manner and often not resolve the customers' issues. However, it's important to assess the differences between onshore and offshore in this regard so that it provides useful insight into whether call centres are better to be offshored or kept at home. If to achieve the same percentage of first call resolutions, the average handle time is 50% more than an onshore centre, then you have wiped out much of the cost savings even before you consider other factors.

The only ways to solve this issue is through the effective implementation of coaching and training strategies specifically designed to combat this. Many of the more professional call centres in The Philippines have already done this and brought average handle time to a very similar level to that of domestic centres. You should be careful to ensure that any strategies designed to reduce the average handle time are based on increasing the communication skills of the customers and are not adversely impact your customers.

Straight to Resolution

"Straight to resolution" is an issue with offshore call centre agents in many countries but I've found it to be a major issue with Filipino agents if they are not trained correctly to deal with it. "Straight to resolution" is the scenario where an agent hears the initial communication from the caller, they believe they understand the customer's issue and then seek to address this issue without necessarily fully comprehending the full issue. This factor is especially true when the standard of English is not up to the required standards but can even be an issue even with agents who have passed strict language assessments. This issue is addressed through more stringent assessment processes in the recruitment process and through on-going training and coaching programs.

Different vendors have adopted different strategies in assessing the level of English within their applicants including computer based assessments and the use of expats to conduct the assessments. A number of human resources personnel have complained that the need to find large volumes of agents within limited timeframes has led them to reduce standards of English competency to meet these demands. This damages the reputation of the company and the wider industry within the country.

Specific Language Issues

There are a number of issues with the way in which many Filipinos speak English which are often as a result of the differences between Tagalog and English. Although the alphabets of English & Tagalog are almost the same, there are a number of grammatical differences between the two languages. For example, some Filipinos have issues with uncountable nouns and you will often hear Filipinos trying to pluralise such as changing "data" to "datas". Like other Austronesian languages, Tagalog is a gender-neutral language. This is why you will often find Filipino referring to men as women and vice-versa. People within the industry will generally tell you that these issues will not be faced in Philippine call centres due to the education and screening of the agents. However, I can assure you that in many centres, these basic grammatical errors are widespread.

British and Australian Accents

The English learnt by Filipinos either through formal education or by the extensive watching of English language television shows is predominantly American English. They are far less exposed to the vocabulary, phraseology and accent of residents of countries such as The UK and Australia and the increase in call centre traffic originating from these countries has caused additional issues for some Philippine based centres. A number of call centres have implemented additional training courses to deal with these issues and these have produced positive results when implemented correctly. There are a number of external training providers who now offer courses to assist with British and Australian accents and many vendors with substantial call centre traffic from these countries often have employ British and Australian nationals within their operations.

English Only

Most call centres operate an "English-only" policy in their operations area where agents are prohibited from speaking in native languages such as Tagalog. There are a number of reasons why they adopt this policy. For example, it is felt that it could be off-putting to a caller if they can hear foreign languages in the background. It's also believed that by agents speaking English as much of the time as possible, this can only enhance their language skills. Similar policies are adopted in other offshore call centre locations including in India.

Falling Standards

The rapid and vast expansion of the call centre sector means that companies are recruiting from increasingly diverse graduate labour pools where English is not as widely spoken. Improvements in both the Government education system and that of English-languages courses offered by private firms have addressed this issue to an extent but with continued expansion of the sector, there is an on-going battle to meet the English language demands. The Philippines clearly has a natural advantage over other locations in terms of spoken English and the majority of the industry has been able to maintain high standards but it must be a significant issue for any client when selecting a specific vendor.

Chapter 4

Managing Filipinos

"Communication styles, relationship bonds & even values are different in Filipino culture and understanding these are crucial to the success in bringing out the best in Filipino call centre agents and managers".

In almost every article promoting The Philippines as a call centre destination, the opinion is stated that Filipinos are culturally similar to Westerners especially Americans. This statement is highly simplistic and to a large extent misleading. There are a number of factors where there are cultural similarities but when it comes to business and managing Filipinos, there are many differences. The subject of maximising the potential of Filipinos could fill an entire book on its own but this chapter provides some specific examples of the differences in managing Filipinos in a contact centre environment.

Agents Follow Their Team Leaders

I'm sure many people who've worked in call centres in The UK or The USA have met team-leaders who think that when they leave, the whole operation will fall down without them and that his or her team will leave soon after. Of course, unless there is some underlying cause for this, it rarely happens but In The Philippines, it's actually widespread. The nature of Filipinos often means that co-workers form strong bonds and this happens across the organisation structure and many of them will follow their line managers to their next job opportunity. This strong bond has another side effect which is often overlooked. Team-leaders, coaches and quality control staff often build up a relationship over time which can often make it harder for them to do their job effectively. In 2002, I visited a centre in Manila which was experiencing quality issues with one of their clients. I suggested to the operations director that he did a quick restructure so that team-leaders would manage different teams. The account included 7 team-leaders and my untested theory was that each of these 7 should be allocated to agents whom they knew the least well. It's true to say that there was some resistance to the idea from both team-leaders and agents but the results were immediate, dramatic and long-standing. Each team leader quickly noticed things that their new agents were doing things wrong and were able to make some pretty significant improvements. I then suggested that this should be something which should be done a fairly regular basis and even to switch agents across different accounts where feasible. Based on my new found wisdom, I then worked with a number of other centres and got them to adopt a similar approach and all experienced positive results. Although we never measured it, I'm sure that the number of agents who followed their team-leaders to their next company also reduced dramatically. Similar caution is also needed when allocating quality control analysts to specific agents.

Pizza Over Cash

When running a telesales operation in Manila, a client of mine came to The Philippines with his pockets stuffed with 500 peso notes. He wanted to create a buzz around the office by giving out on the spot incentives. The money that some of the agents made was about the equivalent of 2 weeks net salary. The client flew home the day after these incentives were given out armed with the "knowledge" that he'd worked out how to motivate Filipinos. At the end of the shift, the floor supervisor told me that one of the team-leaders wanted a holiday for the next day and he was going to grant him this. When I questioned the supervisor about the merits of this, he pointed out that he thought a number of the agents wouldn't come in the following day. Feeling rather perplexed by this, I had one of the rare moments in my life where I didn't have anything to say. Sure enough, absenteeism was very high the next day with the top-performers not showing up. In fact, some of them didn't show up for 3 days. After his long flight home, the client received his report of the results for the day after he'd left and was shocked to see how his total sales had plummeted by 50% within 1 day. The moral of the story is that foreigners should never assume that they know better than their Filipino counterparts about what motivates Filipinos. Immediate cash incentives can be a solution to improve sales but you should always check the merits or disadvantages about anything you plan to introduce with local management. This isn't just important for incentive schemes but for all ways of getting the best performance out of your employees.

On the client's next trip, I took him out to lunch with the supervisor who I'd previously asked to come up with a special incentive and for him to explain the idea before we'd even got to the office. The plan was that each team which hit their total team targets would go out to the finest pizza restaurant in the area. The result was that every team hit the targets and the best agents still turned up for work the following day. Filipinos love social interaction and the lure of the pizza party was enough to get them excited. I've also found that Filipinos are typically far less cynical about any kind of incentive schemes than their counterparts in the many British call centres that I've worked in and a relatively small amount of money can have a dramatic impact if implemented correctly.

Implementing Change

One area of Filipino work culture which often surprises Westerners is the way in which they choose to respond to a change in their working environment. I learnt this when we had to change the shift patterns of some agents so that they worked 1 in every 3 Saturdays and would have a day off in the week instead. Of course, this would be an issue in any call centre in the world but it was something we had to do. I took the agents into a room and explained the situation and even brought pizza which always seems obligatory when trying to win support from Filipinos. At the end of the meeting, nobody raised any concerns and I left the room surprised at how easy it had been. Several hours later, a shift supervisor informed me that I had a near-mutiny on my hands as the changes hadn't been accepted in the way I'd thought. There are several lessons here. The obvious one is that Filipinos don't like confrontation especially with those higher up in the organisation and especially if they're foreigners. Just because they don't raise their concerns doesn't mean that they don't have concerns. It's also true that I should have discussed the way for communicating this message with the Filipino management within the organisation to determine how they would approach this situation. It's worth repeating the message that Filipinos know better than foreigners how to manage and communicate with other Filipinos and their advice should always be sought in such situations.

The Importance of Family

Even with a small insight into Philippine culture, it will be apparent that the role of family is core to the way that Philippine society operates. However, what might not be clear is the way in which the role of family impacts work-life in so many ways. For example, the salaries of call centre workers are often being used to pay for the younger siblings to go through college. In 2007-8, there was a global rice crisis where rice exporting countries such as Vietnam and India restricted their rice exports. Like much of Asia, rice is the most important staple food for Filipinos and there was increasing panic about whether the rice-importing Philippines would be able to cope. To combat this, a number of call centre companies purchased rice which they would then provide to their staff and their families. It's quite amazing what a positive impact such a small gesture made. The call centre agents quite simply became heroes within their families just with a few bags of rice. This situation reminded me of a conversation I had with a Filipino priest shortly after I received in Manila. He told me that Filipinos juggle 4 balls in their lives; their family, their health, their god and their work. Of the 4 balls, only the work ball is made of rubber and will bounce if you drop it. The other 3 balls are made of glass and will smash once dropped. I guess this thought process isn't unique to Filipinos but it does highlight the importance of family to Filipinos.

Chismis

"Chismis" is a commonly used word in the Taglog language which translates to "gossip" in English. It's no surprise that "chismis" is one of the first words foreigners learn in The Philippines because its use is so widespread. The call centre environment in any country lends itself to a culture of gossip and rumour mainly due to the large number of young people working in close proximity and the rapid way in which things can change in such an environment. However, in The Philippines, I have often been shocked at the amount of "chismis" and the speed with which it spreads. One time, I worked with a client who operated across multiple vendors in Metro Manila. The client was introducing widespread changes to the project and it was my job to communicate these changes to the agents. By the time, I'd arrived at the second call centre, the agents had already been pre-warned about the changes but the inevitable Chinese-whispers had altered some of the key messages and whilst the changes were predominantly positive, they'd been communicated to the agents at the second centre with a very negative twist. It had taken me less than an hour from when I'd finished communicating to the first set of agents to speak with the second set but the traffic in Manila moves far slower than text messages! It's very difficult to control such gossiping among call centre agents. Most centres already ban the use of mobile phones on the operations floor already but this doesn't prevent them from texting on their breaks. In fact, the issue is not one you can approach through restricting communication but you should be far clearer in the communication process. Many experts prefer to document all changes and ensure the agents have this available to read in addition to or instead of verbally communicating the changes. Chismis certainly isn't unique to call centres. Filipinos use social media and text messaging heavily to discuss everything from politics to work. You can't change this but you do need to ensure that your messages are received loud and clear. You also need to provide a culture of trust within your organisation so that the Filipinos don't fear negative rumours.

The Devil is in The Detail

Many senior executives of outsourcing companies believe that their Filipino staff are very strong when it comes to following well-documented processes but can be weaker than their counterparts in onshore call centres when it comes to critical thinking. Sometimes, this means that an operations manual designed for use in The United States or United Kingdom needs further clarifications when used in The Philippines or other offshore locations. On the positive side, this can mean that Filipino agents are often strong in adhering with compliance-related issues but it may also mean that they need more regimented call scripts as opposed to call guides. When implementing this, it's essential that this still results in a positive experience for the end customer who have often complained that offshore agents fail to look for creative solutions to their complaints.

Informal or Formal

The many different foreign managers of call centres in The Philippines have many different approaches when it comes to the way in which they engage with their staff. Call centres have to be an enjoyable place to work and this is especially true when working night-shifts as the job tends to take over much of the life of the employees. Newcomers from overseas tend to be overwhelmed with the friendly nature of Filipinos and then feel they need to manage their staff on an over-friendly basis. Many of those who have been working in The Philippines for longer periods of time tend to resort to a more formal approach often believing that over-familiarity can breed contempt. However, I've often seen that the most effective overseas managers tend to combine a mixture of a formal and informal approach. Filipinos respond well to managers who are approachable but they also respect authority and successful managers must acknowledge this. Management styles which work in onshore call centres may therefore need to be modified in The Philippines.

Chapter 5

The Different Types of Contact Centre Work

"There are many different types of service offered in the call centres of The Philippines. Some believe that the only common thing between them is that they involve the use of a telephone but some don't even involve that".

Although this book is entitled call centre outsourcing, the industry covers a wide range of different interaction types. In addition to the typical telephone based communications, there is an increasingly volume of non-voice services offered in contact centres in The Philippines and around the world. Many companies are now also adopting "call reduction strategies" whereby customers are encouraged to communicate with businesses through other methods which should be cheaper for the business to operate. It's also widely believed that non-voice contact centre processes are easier to offshore and The Philippines is obviously one of the beneficiaries of moves in this area. In terms of voice services, The Philippines offers the same range of services that you would expect in any country including customer services, technical support, debt collection and telemarketing activities:

Customer Service

Customer service activities constitute the majority of the work conducted by the large call centre operators in the country and many centres will only work on such accounts. It's true that the Filipinos are a naturally service orientated people which is why this type of activity is so popular. Essentially, customer service agents take calls from customers about a range of enquiries such as issues with a product or service, billing enquiries and order requests. Although not universal, it's common for businesses to keep the high-end or more complex customer service activities onshore and to offshore more basic interaction types. Often, the offshore agent is given less authority than their onshore equivalent and may have to divert the call to a domestically based agent if they are unable to deal with it. Many industry analysts believe that the lack of empowerment of offshore agents is one of the key reasons for consumer dissatisfaction with overseas based call centres.

The level of business satisfaction with Philippine based customer service is high subject to some of the issues I've highlighted in this book and The Philippines continues to take an increased market share of this sector globally. Increasingly, we are seeing more complex types of activities in this area as opposed to simply basic customer service work. For example, companies are now being asked to work on projects where a particular skill is required such as experience in the healthcare industry and I recently worked with a client who needed chemistry graduates for a very specific project. Most customer service activities are business to consumer and it's unusual for a company to offshore business to business customer service activities. Where companies are able to differentiate their high value customers, these tend to be answered by onshore agents. For example, much of HSBC's customer service enquiries are routed to offshore call centres whereas their premier customers are always answered within domestic centres.

Outbound

It's generally accepted that the Filipinos are among the politest nations in the world but not necessarily pushy salespeople although foreign visitors to The Greenhills shopping mall in Manila might dispute this after they have been chased round by people trying to sell them handbags. Despite the Filipinos apparent lack of passion for proactive communication, a large amount of outbound calling is conducted from The Philippines. Many of the companies who use business to consumer outbound services have switched from providers in India to The Philippines for the same reasons that customer service work has been moved.

Outbound covers a wide range of different applications from surveys to telesales and there are some areas such as telecommunications where The Philippines takes a disproportionately large amount of the overall market. As opposed to customer service work where the work is almost always paid for on a per agent hour or per FTE per month basis, outbound is often paid for by results or a combination of an hourly rate with a results-based component. For example, much of the customer acquisition work in the telecommunications sector is undertaken on a purely commission-only basis. A lack of appetite for this type of work from onshore centres has pushed this type of work to offshore locations. A number of laws have been enacted in Western countries to improve the image of outbound telemarketing. In The United States, operators must comply with the "Do Not Call (DNC) List" which means that someone can opt out of receiving telemarketing calls from companies with whom they have no relationship. In The United Kingdom, "The Telephone Preference Services" operate a similar system. The UK also has strict laws governing the use of silent calls by predictive dialing equipment. In 2011, the British telecommunications company "Talk Talk" was found to have breached these laws and they blamed these failings on their outsourced vendors in South Africa. It's widely believed that many Philippines-based vendors flout these laws based on the misunderstanding that these provisions do not apply to them. Given that the client is the company against whom legal proceedings will be taken, they will increasingly look to ensure their vendors comply with all relevant legislation and this is likely to change the way many operators work.

Technical Support

If there's one area of voice based call centre services where India still dominates, it's in the technical support arena. The Indians pride themselves on their large IT Outsourcing industry and the educational system which provides the talent pool for ITO is equally as successful in producing high-calibre technical support agents. That's not to say there isn't an opportunity for Philippine based centres and there are plenty of examples where The Philippines has been selected over India for such work. The Philippines clearly wants to increase its share of higher value outsourcing work and believe that the perception of its superior English skills coupled with improvements in some areas of the education system will enable them to do so. There are a number of outsourced vendors who specialise in technical support in Manila and they've been very successful in winning and delivering high quality business. The increased cost of employing this level of people in India means that The Philippines can certainly compete on cost. In fact, it's clear that if you need to recruit 50 technical support personnel in Manila, you can easily find them and the costs are comparable to India. Whilst it's uncertain whether The Philippines technical support industry will match India in terms of size, most companies looking at outsourcing this type of activity examine vendors in both countries and the fact that the overall size of the current market is smaller in The Philippines is rarely an influencing factor in the procurement process.

Debt Collection and Recoveries

The often passive nature of Filipinos led many people to believe that The Philippines would not be an ideal location for debt collection and recoveries work and the feedback from clients operating in these areas have been mixed. This is primarily due to the fact that collections is a complex and difficult application to master. It requires a mixture of good process with the right people and just because an operation is proficient in customer services activities does not mean that they can automatically do collections work. Companies such as IQOR & NCO are specialists in these areas and have large numbers of people in multiple locations in The Philippines and have been very successful. Some others who specialise in customer service have also been successful at collections in The Philippines but they've adopted specific recruitment and management processes to make it work. One example of this is Allsec Technologies who are a general call centre vendor but have brought skills and expertise in collections from their Indian operations and found the Filipinos highly successful at this type of activity. Many companies believe that offshore operations should be used for older debt where it is no longer economically viable to collect on these portfolios in domestic operations.

Non-voice call centre services

One of the major issues often associated with India is that of the accent and the majority of industry experts believe that The Philippines has a natural advantage over India in this area. Of course, this is not an issue in areas where voice is not required such as in email support, web chat and in social media interactions. As a result of this, there are some companies which had previously outsourced all of their contact centre activity to India but then decided to move their voice work to The Philippines who left the non-voice portion in India.

Many global companies are increasingly offering innovative solutions to their clients to enable their customers to analyse social media channels and to interact with them in this way. It is believed that customers will have less resistance to offshoring non-voice activities than they do through voice channels and so The Philippines wants to have their share of these opportunities. Overall, the primary interaction channel is still through the telephone but we will see more and more companies expand their non-voice offerings. There are already a small number of Philippines based companies offering exclusively non-voice contact centre services and I expect this number to grow in line with the growth of these channels. There are also some examples of companies processing letters and order forms through Philippine contact centres. This typically involves the communication being high-speed scanned in the country of origin and then accessed via the internet in The Philippines and then input by data entry agents. This type of work offers relatively low margins compared with voice based services and the agents doing this work will typically earn lower salaries than their voice-based equivalents. It is for the same reason that this type of work is often done outside Metro Manila where costs are even lower.

Chapter 6

The different types of vendors & Operating Models

"The call centre industry is highly complex involving many different types of organisation operating under vastly different operating models"

There are now a multitude of call centres across The Philippines varying from the very small to the vast call centres operated by the international players. With such a vast array of vendors, it's important to recognise that there are many different types of centre operating in a variety of ways. They differ greatly in size, pricing, technology, management infrastructure, ownership and the type of work they undertake. There are 7 different types of vendor currently operating within The Philippines as follows:

(1) The large international players. These include companies such as SITEL, Teletech, Teleperformance and pretty much every major call centre outsourcing vendor.

(2) Traditional offshore companies. These are predominantly Indian owned outsourcing companies who have expanded into The Philippines due to changing client requirements. All major Indian BPO companies now have a presence in The Philippines which are almost without exception located in Metro Manila. This group includes companies such as 247 Customer. Many of these companies have now grown from being pure-play offshore providers to becoming large international players themselves having acquired facilities in countries such as The United States or by establishing their own facilities there.

(3) Domestic centres. These are Western companies who operate as outsourcing vendors in their own countries and have operations in The Philippines which operate as their exclusive low cost, offshore operation. Most of these are American companies but there are a few Australian & Canadian owned companies too. They differ from the large international players in that they don't operate a global delivery model.

(4) Partnerships between local and foreign entrepreneurs. In the early stages of the offshoring boom, these were common-

place. These are partnerships between foreign companies (either entrepreneurs or small to medium sized American call centre vendors) & a local partner who would either be a wealthy Philippine entrepreneur or business.

(5) Philippine owned entities. These are normally owned by wealthy Filipinos with other business interests who establish their own outsourced company. They are effectively the same as the partnerships detailed above but without an international partner.

(6) Micro call centres. These are very small call centres which are owned by small-scale entrepreneurs. They are mostly Filipino-owned but there are also some owned by foreign entrepreneurs.

(7) Specialist operators. These are centres which specialise in either providing very specific services such as technical support or provide services exclusively to a particular industry.

The Large International Players

The large international call centre operators all have a substantial presence in The Philippines. These include Convergys, Teletech, Sykes, Aegis & Teleperformance and it is not unusual for them to have in excess of 10,000 call centre agents in the country. Their largest bases tend to be in Metro Manila and they often source through recruitment fairs across the country. Many of them also have operations in other cities around the country. Their operating procedures and the technologies they use tend to be very similar to those deployed in their other centres around the world. Their services are typically sold through business development teams who will sell all of the geographies they operate in but each sales person is usually allocated to specific industries. These business development teams are backed by support functions in The Philippines who will facilitate site visits and will often be involved in the lead generation process.

The Philippines will typically be one of their largest facilities they operate anywhere in the world. Most of them service almost all industry sectors and provide a broad range of call centre services. The largest section of this work will normally be customer services work and many choose not to take on projects in outbound telemarketing, debt collection or technical support. This group tends to have a higher cost base than smaller vendors as they are more likely to have leading edge technologies, higher office specifications and larger management structures. As a result, their pricing structures will typically be at a premium to smaller operations and tend to be either on a cost per agent hour or cost per agent per month basis.

They will often employ international managers for senior operational and training roles. In some circumstances, the technology for these companies is managed on a global scale which is usually outside of The Philippines. Client management is performed through a combination of Philippine based resources and resources based in the client's own country. The Philippines-based client management teams tend to perform basic functions such as report production and communicating information to operations teams. High-end client management functions such as strategic reviews are usually performed in the client's own country. As the industry has matured and the skills of the Filipinos have improved, many international vendors have tried to push more and more client facing functions to The Philippines where costs are substantially lower. It's very common for companies in this group to have a number of internationally recognised accreditations covering areas such as data security and quality procedures. Some of the more common accreditations include ISO:9001, ISO:27001, PCI DSS & COPC. Even some of those vendors who do not operate such accreditations within their domestic centres do so offshore in the belief that they must provide a number of reassurances to their clients offshore that wouldn't necessarily be required onshore.

Traditional Offshore Companies

A number of companies established themselves specifically to provide offshore call centre services due to the larger operating margins compared with domestic centres. Many of these companies were founded in India but have either bought or established Philippine operations due to strong client demand. There are a large number of these companies in The Philippines and they tend to operate medium to large scale operations which are normally located in Metro Manila. For many of them, The Philippines is now either their largest operation or second in size to India. In line with industry trends, their operations in The Philippines have normally been growing faster than their locations in India or elsewhere. They are similar to large international players in their sales process, the technology they deploy and the standard of their operations. Their pricing is similar to international players although sometimes with a slight cost reduction reflecting their smaller management hierarchies. Some of these vendors will specialise in another type of outsourcing such as IT Outsourcing but have branched out into offering call centre services and other forms of business process outsourcing. These companies will often win business from clients for whom they provide their main services. HCL and Infosys are two prime examples of this.

Philippine Owned Entities

The growth of the call centre industry attracted a number of The Philippines' entrepreneurs into the industry and many have invested heavily in operations which are similar or slightly inferior to the capabilities of the large international players. They differ from the international operators in many ways such as their smaller size of operations, lower pricing structures and the way in which they win business. The bulk of these operations offer the full spectrum of call centre services but will many only win outbound telemarketing work where much of this work is paid for on a performance only basis. The high cost of recruiting business development personnel in Western countries means that they often win business through brokers or middlemen and some of them use Filipinos who conduct lead generation calls to potential clients. The brokers operate using a variety of different models. Sometimes, they will contract with the end client and then sub-outsource the work to a call centre after taking their profit margins. Others will organise a contract between the client and the vendor and then charge the call centre a fee for finding the clients which is normally a percentage of the contract value paid on receipt of payment. Brokers tend to deal in low value telemarketing projects where the call centre is normally only paid on a performance basis such as cost per sale. The low barriers to entry to becoming a broker has meant that a large number of unscrupulous individuals have entered this market and many owners of call centres in The Philippines have complained that they struggle to receive payment from these clients.

Domestic/International Partnerships

This type of business model works almost the same as for the Philippine owned entities centres with the exception that there is a foreign business partner who is normally but not always an American. The specific arrangements vary but will normally involve the local partner being responsible for all Philippines based issues such as recruitment, office leases and operations whilst the foreign partner is usually responsible for issues in the client marketplace such as marketing, sales and servicing the client base. The benefit of this approach for The Philippines partner is that it should give them access to prospective client contacts and a business development resource in the country where the clients are. In practice, many of these relationships have broken down due to poor expectation setting and one or both parties believing that they are contributing too much to the partnership. They are still popular but have often failed to yield the results they'd hoped for at the outset.

Micro Call Centres

There are vast numbers of what I refer to as micro call centres across The Philippines. They are generally owned and run by local entrepreneurs and are set up on a shoe-string budget. They tend to gain business through social media platforms such as LinkedIn or through middlemen. They sometimes win business from other centres who recommend them when they don't wish to take on a certain client themselves.

They range in size from 1 call centre agent upwards and there are large numbers of them across The Philippines. They operate on a very low cost base and tend to use free or very cheap call centre technology such as Vicidial.

All processes within these operations such as recruitment, training and performance management tend to be weak but this is reflected in their pricing. Their clients will normally be small businesses but this is not always the case. Despite my negativity towards micro-operators, there are some very good quality vendors who fit into this category. In my experience, the difference between the good and bad micro operators is always the quality of the individual running the company.

Some micro operators also operate using a "call centre hotel" facility. A call centre hotel is an office fitted out with fairly standard call centre technology and furniture. It enables a company to move in very quickly into a facility which is ready to make and receive calls almost immediately with zero or very minimal capital outlay. These call centre hotels normally charge on a cost per seat basis plus the associated telecommunications costs. Call centre hotels will normally house a number of different micro operators on very flexible rental terms. They have also been used by larger operators to enable them to start small or to expand rapidly.

Specialist Operators

Many larger operators divide their business development resources according to a particular business sector but will generally cover all of the main sectors such as Financial Services, Telecommunications, Retail, Utilities and Travel. They will also offer a broad range of services covering all forms of communication including voice and non-voice channels. However, specialist operators set up to service one particular service or business sector. This is generally because the founders of those have very specific knowledge and industry contacts in these markets. This is not unique to The Philippines but there an increasing number of vendors operating in these niche markets.

They employ personnel at all levels with specific knowledge and skill-sets and build their technology platforms to best service these markets. Of course, the fact that they only service a small sector means that they are generally smaller than generic vendors but can charge a premium for their services and often use their specialisation as their differentiator in the sales process. Some vendors have their own domestic operations but have expanded to The Philippines because of the skillsets which exist in the country. Over the next decade, we will see more specialist vendors operating in areas where The Philippines has a natural advantage in areas such as healthcare and technology.

Types of Operating Models

Build Operate Transfers are rare in The Philippines. In the early stages of the offshore call centre boom in India, a number of companies established such agreements. The concept normally involved an outsourced service provider establishing a specific facility for a client either within an existing facility or as a stand-alone facility. This was very popular with companies who preferred to operate their own captive facilities but felt that they needed support when entering a new market such as India. The outsourced service provider would provide the services for a specific time period before the operation was transferred over to the client who would then run it on their own. These agreements have declined in their popularity in India and by the time that offshoring boomed in The Philippines, clients were moving away from such agreements. They had either decided that they could set up their own captive facilities from scratch or felt that outsourcing was a better option.

A more popular concept in The Philippines has been the build-transfer model where a Philippine-owned company would build a facility specifically designed for an outsourced service provider and lease the facility to them. These would normally be based on very long lease periods. A number of the country's leading real estate companies such as Ayala Land & Megaworld have built such facilities and their popularity remains high with large international vendors and international companies wanting to establish their own captive facilities.

The Home Agent Model

In The United States, the work from home agent model has been fairly successful for many operators whilst in The UK, the percentage of agents working in this model is far lower. Offshore, there are very few agents working from home and The Philippines is no exception. There are a number of micro-operators in this field and there are even some individuals who even offer this service on a self-employed basis. However, none of them have been able to do this on any significant scale to date and I don't see this changing in the near future. For many clients of outsourced vendors, outsourcing overseas already represents a significant risk factor and the additional risk of using at-home agents is not a hurdle they wish to cross. Without any facility-related costs, home agents are relatively low cost.

Chapter 7

Locations

"The Philippines boasts a number of large, well-developed Central Business Districts highly suitable for outsourcing companies. Estimates suggest that as much as 2 million square kilometres of office space have been leased to outsourcing companies predominantly in the call centre sector."

When discussing the call centre locations within The Philippines, it's best to consider them in 3 sections:

(1) Metro Manila
(2) Metro Cebu & Clark
(3) The next wave cities

Metro Manila

Metro Manila consists of 16 different cities and the municipality of Pateros. It is already home to over 21 million Filipinos and continues to grow at its population at a rapid rate. Despite Government attempts to increase the popularity of other locations, Metro Manila is still home to the vast majority of the call centres in the country which are predominantly located in the following of its cities:

- Makati City. Makati City is the undisputed leading central business district of Metro Manila and houses many of the country's leading hotels such as The Shangri La and Peninsula. It is also home to The Philippine Stock Exchange and a disproportionately large share of the country's premier office space. In the early stages of industry development, many call centres moved into some of Makati's most prestigious real estate such as The Philam Life Building and RSBC Plaza due to the low rental rates which were offered. After the initial contract periods were up, the landlords hiked the prices forcing call centres to move to more affordable accommodation. Between 2002 & 2007, the cost of premium office space in Makati rose from 400 pesos per square metre to 1000 pesos per square metre per month and in an industry with shrinking margins, this was simply not sustainable. Makati remains a popular destination for call centres and many vendors with multiple locations often use Makati as their showcase site and a number have their own purposed built centres in the city inclusive of restaurants and cafes for their hungry workforce.
- Pasig City. Pasig's primary site for call centres is the Ortigas Center which is a very popular destination. Emerald Avenue

in Ortigas comes to life in the middle of the night when call centre agents head to the restaurants and coffee shops on their lunch-breaks. Rental costs in Ortigas are lower than in Makati at around 600 pesos per square metre and the area is well supported by substantial public transport. Association dues are also lower in Ortigas at around 150 pesos per square metre which is roughly 25% cheaper than in Makati.

- Quezon City has the largest population of all of Metro Mania's cities and is home to many call centres especially in the area known as Eastwood. Eastwood was set up as a PEZA registered location offering substantial tax incentives to locators. Many call centres took space in the offices there and some outsourcing vendors such as Epixtar and C-Cubed had their own designated buildings. Eastwood has expanded significantly to include restaurants and hotels including the Eastwood Richmonde Hotel which houses many foreigners when visiting their outsourced partners. Outside of Eastwood, there are also a large number of call centres in other parts of Quezon City who have been attracted by the relative proximity of a large labour force.

- Taguig City. Taguig is home to The Fort Bonifacio which is a modern development consisting of many offices in addition to leisure and retail establishments. Call centre space is relatively expensive at close to 800 pesos per square metre reflecting the high specifications of the buildings located there.

- Muntilupa City. Muntilupa is another call centre hotspot in Metro Manila especially in the district of Alabang. Rental prices are relatively low at just over 500 pesos per square metre but still offer such attractive and high specification accommodation highly suitable for call centres.

Metro Cebu & Metro Clark

The Metro Clark and Metro Cebu areas have significant call centre populations. Costs in these 2 locations can be lower than Metro Manila due to lower property and wage costs. However, when calculating these costs back to a "per agent hour" basis, the savings are counted in cents rather than dollars. The centres in Cebu are generally owned either by local entrepreneurs or are additional facilities for the international vendors who also operate in Manila. Cebu has similar issues to Manila in terms of the tightness of its labour pool. Some estimates suggest that Cebu is 15% cheaper than Metro Manila but this conflicts with industry executives that I have spoken with who suggest total costs are far closer.

The Metro Clark area continues to be a popular call centre location. Clark was the home for a large United States Air Force base until 1991. The departure of the Air Force created a black hole in terms of employment in the area and it was designated as a special economic zone offering financial incentives to firms setting up in the area. These incentives coupled with an abundance of English speaking personnel led a number of small and mid-sized operators to establish a presence there.

Next Wave Cities

The rest of the country has traditionally been a major recruiting pool for centres based in Manila. Some centres have even conducted highly successful recruitment initiatives in specific cities in the hope of attracting residents of these smaller cities to live and work in Manila. However, the country believes that it can only continue to expand its outsourcing sector if vendors establish operations in these smaller cities. It has therefore initiated a series of initiatives to ensure these cities have the correct infrastructure to be able to support outsourcing jobs. These cities offer discounts to Metro Manila in salaries and the cost of real estate. These so-called "next-wave cities" are as follows:

1. Davao City. Davao is the largest city in the south of the country with a population of approximately 1.5 million people with a total of 2.3 million people in the wider Metro Davao area. Of these cities, Davao has the largest volume of both call centres and call centre agents. As of 2012, the city had a call centre agent population of roughly 16,000 but there are plans to expand this to over 40,000. The company is already home to some of the world's leading call centre operators such as SITEL, Aegis, ETelcare (Stream) and a number of smaller operators. The city has an abundance of office accommodation suitable for contact centre operations.

2. Santa Rosa City. Santa Rosa is itself a small city with a population of under 300,000 people. It benefits from its relative proximity to Metro Manila and can be reached by road in about 2 hours. It has a small number of call centre agents currently but does offer substantial discounts in salary & real estate costs and attrition amongst the current call centres are believed to be lower than in the larger conurbations. Convergys are among the call centre vendors already operating in Santa Rosa where there is a good road system along with suitable power and telecommunications infrastructure and has sites available for PEZA incentives

3. Bacolod City. Located in The Central Philippines, the population is just over half a million people. There are already a small number of centres there but its industry is very small in comparison even with Clark or Cebu. Convergys have 2 call centres in Bacolod located in buildings next to each other. Other major providers in the city include Teletech, Transcom and Teleperformance. Tholons rank Bacolod as the 94th most suitable outsourcing destination in the world

4. Iloilo City. Iloilo has a population of 1.8 million people. A number of call centres operated there including locally owned and foreign companies. Teletech have a sizeable operation in the city. Iloilo City has the lowest average wage, rental and

power rates among the next wave cities. The city is also ranked in Tholons top 100 outsourcing destinations.

5. Metro Cavite. Convergys are one of a number call centre operators in Cavite. Cavite is located close to Manila's high density university belt providing an excellent labour supply coupled with low rental costs.

6. Lipa City. Lipa City is located in Batangas a few hours' drive away from Manila. It is home to just over 200,000 people and has a fairly small call centre industry. It boasts a good road structure and telecommunications infrastructure.

7. Cagayan de Oro City. With over 600,000 inhabitants, Cagayon De Oro is one of the largest cities in Mindanao. Just like other cities in the area such as Davao, it is often tarred with being in an unstable part of the country and this has deterred many of the international call centre players. The city offers some of the lowest costs of any of the next wave cities.

8. Malolos City. Malalos is like a number of other small cities in the Luzon area who believe that the low cost base for real estate and wages can attract outsourcing vendors away from nearby Manila. Unfortunately, it has not done so on any significant scale to date

9. Baguio City. SITEL operates large call centre in The Baguio City Enterprise Zone. In addition to SITEL, there are a number of smaller operators across the city and also global giant Aegis. Baguio is ranked by Tholons as the 99th most suitable outsourcing location in the world.

10. Dumaguete City. As a small city in the central Philippines, the call centre industry is relatively small but it is known as the "center of learning in the south" with a number of highly respected educational institutions in the city.

Chapter 8

Infrastructure & Technology

"The problem with the Philippines was that in the provinces you have rivers with no bridges and a metropolitan Manila that has bridges with no rivers" - *President Gloria Macapagal Arroyo*

The quote about the bridges might seem an unusual one for a President to make about her own country but this is what she said during a conversation with Martin Conboy, a well-respected Australian outsourcing guru. What the former President meant by this was that a disproportionate amount of infrastructure spending in The Philippines occurred in The Metro Manila area. Metro Manila clearly has the infrastructure required for outsourcing companies otherwise they would not have come in their droves but there are concerns that the infrastructure in some provinces is not suitable. For the industry is to keep expanding, an ever-increasing percentage of the call centre population need to be outside of the capital. This "revelation" will not come as a revelation to BPAP's executives or Government officials who have been trying to encourage outsourcing and offshoring. The Government has also made a number of changes to legislation in order to encourage foreign investors in infrastructure projects and across the next wave cities, infrastructure is improving.

Telecommunications

Telephony in the Philippines is among the most stable in the Asia Pacific region and the growth of the call centre sector has helped to improve this. The cost of bandwidth has gone dramatically. In 2001, an E1 line to The United States cost $14,000 per month and is now a fraction of that. International leased circuits can be delivered in 30-45 days. It used to be difficult to get an estimated delivery time and the schedule you would receive would almost certainly be missed. There is also a wide choice of carriers for local "Last Mile" telecommunications delivery including PLDT, Eastern, Bayantel & Globe. VOIP is widely used in Philippine call centres and is stable if configured correctly. There are a wide range of providers for the delivery of international services from BT, C&W, AT&T and Verizon all having resilient infrastructure across separate PoPs. There are also multiple submarine cable routes into the Philippines.

Power

Power-outages in The Philippines were common place in the last century and at the start of this. Call centres are typically power-hungry facilities especially in The Philippines where the climate means air-conditioning is essential in all office spaces and areas housing servers and technology equipment. Continuity of service is essential for call centre servicing and as a result, all large outsourcer providers and many of the smaller ones will have their own back-up power facilities. The Aquino administration has earmarked substantial funds for additional power plants in the country.

Technology Providers & Support Infrastructure

Since the start of the offshoring boom, the technology maturity level has significantly increased and is now on par with India. The international call centre technology providers experience all have a significant presence in The Philippines. These include Cisco, Avaya, Variant, NICE and Genesys. Although distributors carry equipment stock delays have been known by call centres and this needs to be factored into to any project. Many companies complain that delivery times increase dramatically in the pre and post-Christmas periods.

Transportation

The Philippines has some rail transit already within The Metro Manila are but everyone including Government officials will tell you that they are lacking behind cities of a similar size and funds have been earmarked for its expansion. Many call centre workers will use jeepneys to get to work which are a highly decorated, low cost minibus service. The costs for these are minimal at around $.025 for a 3 mile journey. Most importantly, the public transport system operates during the times when call centre workers go to and from work. Although the public transport system might seem chaotic to a newcomer, it functions adequately. Outside of Manila, jeepneys and trikes are commonly used.

Flooding

The Philippines does suffer from tropical storms and major flooding can be a major issue as a result. Metro Manila is not immune to flooding and disaster recovery plans to deal with such occurrences should always be considered. However, many Westerners have been amazed at the resilience of their Filipino workforce who have still been able to get to work during periods of heavy rain. Since offshoring boomed in the country, there have been a number of major storms but very few centres have recorded any significant downtime as a result. The Government has given the green light for a 350 Billion peso flood defence system but this isn't due to be operational until 2035. The wet season is June to October and many clients try to avoid visiting their vendors during this period.

Office Accommodation

There is no shortage of suitable call centre accommodation within Manila. In the next wave cities, there has been a growth of office space specifically designed for outsourcing companies.

Chapter 9

Pricing

"Labour arbitrage is the main driver for offshoring call centre work but The Philippines could never win in a race to the lowest price. It must retain the balance between cost and quality to continue its phenomenal success"

The main driver for the rise in offshore call centres has always been the substantially lower costs in comparison with domestically based operations. Between 2000 and 2001, I worked alongside a number of the world's leading consulting firms to help companies establish outsourced vendors in The Philippines. Without exception, every consulting firm said that the price for a productive agent hour in The Philippines should be US$15 and for British customers, the price should be £10. This was based on basic customer services with additional costs for specific skill or language requirements. At the time, these rates were slightly higher than in India but significantly lower than operators in The United States or United Kingdom. Despite rising wage bills and increased real estate costs, these costs have actually come down over the past decade. Premium operators typically charge $11-14 with lower costs for smaller and lower-tiered operators. This chapter examines how these prices are arrived at, what should be expected for these prices and how rates have gone done despite rising costs. On a per employee basis, centres look to make around US$1900 (GB£1250) per month.

For those not involved in call centre outsourcing, the idea of paying $15 or even $12 can seem rather high. A simple maths calculation would say that if you're paying 16000 pesos per month to an agent and they are 160 working hours in the month, then even if the exchange rate went as low as 40 pesos to the dollar, then that's only $2.50 per hour. However, there are a number of factors to consider such as the following:

- You typically pay for a productive hour so you're only paying for the time an agent is ready and able to make or receive calls so even if the agent is paid for 160 hours per month, the client is billed for somewhere between 120-140 hours.

- There are a number of social costs in addition to the salary such as holiday pay, additional pay for holidays etc. Philippines employees are also entitled to 13th month pay

- The cost of recruitment and training is also normally absorbed by the vendor.

- There are also many other people who you're not being charged for such as the trainers, quality control assistants, team-leaders, management, HR etc. Their costs are effectively bundled up into the per agent hour cost.

- There are also costs associated with the facility such as the purchase of technology, office furniture, rental fees, association dues, software licenses etc. etc.

- Lastly, let's not forget that the call centre needs to make a profit even after they've absorbed their own marketing costs.

When we consider all of the above, it's still impossible to give an exact figure as to how much it costs each vendor to "produce" an agent hour before their margin is added but here are some rough ideas how it works:

- The cost price for a strong operator with good training, technology, management, office space & people is in the region of $10-12 per agent hour. BPAP research from 2010 suggests that the cost per employee per year is between $15-16,000 per annum. When calculating this back to a productive hour basis, this is slightly lower than my research but BPAP's figures do not include a variety of components.

- A very basic micro-operator with cheap rental premises, basic staff provision, minimal technology based in the provinces operates at a cost base of about $4 per hour.

- The cost price for a mid-tiered vendor is in the region of $8-9 per agent hour.

Of course, these costs assume a high level of occupancy and do not include the margin for the vendor. Some companies may be operating on a cost base even higher than $12 especially if they have specific skill-set requirements for their agents, occupy premium office space or operate on very low agent to management ratios. The only time when it would be feasible to charge less than $4 is for single agents working on their own from home who are being paid direct by a client. There are a very small number of these but it's very difficult to control data security and to manage such a small operation from 1000's of miles away. There are now so many outsourced vendors in The Philippines that it's possible to find an operator to fit any requirements. There is definitely a trade-off between quality and price and when discussing prices, it's important to ensure you are comparing on a like for like basis.

The practice of price dumping is not uncommon in The Philippine call centre industry. Price dumping is the practice of charging rates lower than the production cost. This is used in a number of situations such as by new vendors trying to obtain their first client, after a vendor has lost a significant client and wants to retain staff or when a vendor wants to expand. By its very nature, price dumping is only something which can take place for a fixed period of time and the majority of clients who have selected a vendor who has "price dumped" to win the business ends up regretting their decision or changing the contractual terms.

Salary Costs

Although salaries are a lower percentage of total operating costs with an offshore facility, they still represent a significant portion. Basic monthly salaries within The Philippines are estimated as follows with all costs quoted in Philippine Pesos (PHP):

• Call Centre Agent (entry level) - PHP13,000-16,000. Some call centres also offer food and transport allowances

• Team Leaders - PHP 25,000- PHP 40,000

• Operations Managers – PHP 50,000 – PHP 100,000 depending on the size of the operation

• Trainers – PHP 20,000 – PHP 50,000

• Directors such as Chief Financial Officer, Operations Directors and HR Directors PHP 150,000 - PHP 350,000

• Managing Director, PHP 400,000 – PHP 600,000 with more for very large operators

The Changing Prices

When the call centre industry really started to accelerate, there was sudden upsurge in wage inflation. Between 2004 & 2005, agent salaries rose by 16% but fell back to a more manageable 5% by 2006. Wages will continue to rise at a similar level for the foreseeable and most importantly, they will rise at a level faster than their counterparts in The United States or United Kingdom. To keep wage inflation under control, The Philippine Government and industry must ensure that the supply of quality labour can keep up with demand. Of course, salary inflation is measured in pesos but a more realistic method of calculation would be for it to be done in dollars. The currency has fluctuated dramatically over the course of the past 13 years. The peso has increased its value by 40% against the dollar between 2004 & 2013. These figures are even worse for British companies. The British Pound was worth 109 pesos in 2004 compared with just over 60 pesos in 2013. Real estate costs have soared but are still lower than India in comparable business districts. Real estate prices in areas such as Makati have soared and to keep costs under control, outsourcing companies have increasingly moved outside of central business districts and even outside Metro Manila.

The common question I'm asked is if costs seem to be going up in The Philippines, why have costs to the clients of outsourcing companies gone down? There are a number of reasons behind this. Firstly, margins have shrunk to similar levels in The United States due to competition. Prior to 2003, margins for offshore call centres were more than double that in domestic centres but have seen a gradual decline to the point now where there is little room for manoeuvre. The larger call centres have also been able to benefit from economies of scale. This is especially true for those vendors who have been successful in attracting business from around the world as they spread their fixed costs over multiple shifts. The cost of telecommunications has also plummeted and the quality of internet connections has improved. As a percentage of total workforce, there are now less foreign managers in call centres who are expensive resources compared with their local equivalents.

Other Pricing Models

Although a per agent hour or per month basis remain the most common pricing mechanisms in both domestic and offshore outsourcing, some types of work are paid for using alternative structures. For example, much of the retail sector charges on a cost per call or cost per call minute basis. The cost per minute varies but will usually be in the range of $0.45 - $0.60 per call minute offering a substantial discount on US call centres. In the outbound sector, work is often priced on a performance basis. In telesales, the work is priced on a cost per sale or a combination of a cost per hour basis plus commission. In areas such as list checking where the agent makes outbound calls to verify contact details, this is often charged on a cost per completed basis. Many contractual agreements include clauses that payment is altered based on pre-specified key performance indicators.

The Future

The Philippines needs to remain competitive on price but at the same time, it should not try to engage in the "race to the bottom" strategy adopted by many countries in low-end manufacturing jobs. Inflation in The Philippines has been running at slightly higher rates than in Western countries due to its rapidly expanding economy. The strength of the peso against the dollar has helped to keep wage inflation down but it is still becoming more expensive in dollar terms. For The Philippines to remain a competitive destination, it needs to ensure that inflation is kept under control and its currency does not appreciate too rapidly. Outsourcing business Genpact are quoted as saying that costs in The Philippines are 4-5% higher than in India which is fairly insignificant in the overall scheme of things. However, Benedict Hernandez, president of the Business Processing Association of the Philippines believes the strong local currency has made the Philippines 30% more expensive than India for outsourcing clients. The country's central bank, Bangko Sentral ng Pilipinas has announced that it is to continue to purchase dollars in an attempt to stop the rise of the peso.

Chapter 10

Beyond The United States

"Over-exposure to the US market is a risk to the vibrancy of The Philippine call centre marketplace. Economic uncertainty & political rhetoric against offshoring have encouraged call centres to look at markets beyond The United States and there has been no shortage of willing clients".

The UK & Australia

Approximately 70% of the total demand for The Philippines call centre industry comes from The United States. Although figures were not produced in the early stages of the industry, it's believed that this figure is actually coming down with unofficial estimates suggesting that it was in excess of 90% at one point. The UK is the second largest market for The Philippines at just under 10%. The remaining 20% comes from a mixture of work from Asia Pacific (where the largest market is Australia), other parts of Europe and local demand within the domestic Philippine marketplace. Although there are some centres which specialise specifically in work coming from places such as The UK or Australia, most centres will offer their services to all English speaking geographies and to some extent, this can help with seat utilisation. With peak call traffic often in daytime hours in the country from which the calls are coming from (or being called), the time zone differences can mean a seat can be used for a US and an Australian shift. However, many vendors prefer to allocate workstations to a specific client and not allow other clients to occupy those stations at other times of the day. Of course, a large number of the deals going to The Philippines are now part of global deals for which calls are answered from all English speaking countries. In cases such as this, some workstations could potentially be occupied for the entire 24 hour period. In reality, there are many centres where a large proportion of the workstations are now occupied for 16-20 hours per day. This is important given that the set up costs for call centres are high and if these can be absorbed by multiple shifts, then the overall cost of delivery is reduced.

The Cultural Affinity

As The Philippines started to dominate the offshore space for American clients, there was a common misconception emerging that The UK was more suited to offshoring to their former colonies such as India. I remember being sat in a conference where I was told that whilst The United States had a close cultural affinity with The Philippines, the same was true of The UK with India. Like most British nationals who have worked extensively with both Indian and Philippine call centres, I believe this to be untrue. Of course, there are a number of passions which Indian British people share such as curry and cricket and there is also the influence of The UK's large Indian population which has so positively enhanced Britain. The historical ties of the two countries also means that trade between the two countries has existed on a significant scale for a long period of time. However, none of this makes India has any significant impact for making India a more viable call centre destination for British calls than other locations. Of course, one of the legacies of Britain's colonial rule in India is the widespread teaching of English but this doesn't replace the fact that English is far more widely spoken in The Philippines than in India. Indeed, the negative sentiment surrounding Indian call centres which swept The United States was felt in equal measures in The UK. Just like in America, British companies focused a great deal of effort in finding alternative call centre destinations to India and The Philippines was one of those. It's estimated that the number of agents working on US-based accounts is about 350,000, 7 times higher than the 50,000 servicing The UK. However, The United States has a population 5 times the size of The UK and so a British consumer is only slightly less likely to have their call answered in The Philippines than their American equivalent.

In 2006, T-Mobile UK started a pilot with SITEL in Manila for its prepaid mobile service to run alongside a similar campaign they ran with UK-based TSC. T-Mobile were able to achieve almost identical results in terms of their key performance indicators such as customer satisfaction with The Philippines as they were with TSC and at a dramatically reduced cost. T-Mobile quickly rolled out the pilot and by 2007, they employed over 300 agents in Manila. Even more importantly for The Philippines than 300 additional call centre roles was that there was now a major UK brand with a Philippines success story and more and more British companies who perhaps would not have wanted to be the guinea-pig were now rushing to Manila. T-Mobile UK and their rival mobile operator Orange have now merged and the new company Everything Everywhere is a major outsourcer to Philippines based vendors. T-Mobile weren't the first UK company to outsource call centre activity to The Philippines. The directory assistance service 118 118 already had a significant presence in Manila as did HSBC in their captive facilities. Many American-owned companies with a UK subsidiary also used their positive experiences with American customers in The Philippines to justify pushing their UK call centre traffic there too. This included companies such as Vonage, Expedia and American Express. Telemarketing to The UK from The Philippines is also very common and I've worked with British companies who have 100's of call centre agents dialing for them in Manila.

In 2007, The Philippines won The Outsourcing Destination of The Year Award from The National Outsourcing Association (NOA) in The UK. This was by no means the start of The Philippines taking market share in The UK but it represent quite how far The Philippines had come in servicing British businesses. Given that most of the Philippines total outsourcing industry was call centre focused, it's fair to say that this award was testament to the Philippines capacity for call centre work. The UK went on to win this award again in 2009 & 2010 but since then, The Philippines has decided not to participate in this awards program.

Whilst India is still a larger provider of call centre agents for British companies, the same is not true for their Australian counterparts who have dumped Indian vendors in their droves to shift to Manila. The "anywhere but India" approach to procuring call centre services which had started in The United States was now very much taking over in other parts of the English-speaking world including in Australia. Forthright speaking Australian consumers had always struggled with Indian call centres and whilst it's still unclear whether they're perfectly happy with Philippine centres, businesses there seem to believe it's a better option. Australia has one of the highest starting salaries for call centre agents in the world at around AUS$40,000 per year and so offshoring is a hot topic around many Australian boardrooms. In February 2013, The Managing Director of Telstra subsidiary Sensis, John Allan, said that their decision to offshore call centre agents to replace those in Australia would improve service for its customers. Judging by the reaction on social media, this is not a sentiment shared by many of the Australian people. In both Australia & The UK, there has been a media-led backlash against the offshoring of call centre jobs and they generally don't differentiate between those based in India and those in The Philippines. A number of high profile companies in both The UK & Australia have publicly stated their opposition to offshoring call centres in any location. This stand seems to be popular with the public at large but there is no evidence to suggest that significant numbers of people have switched suppliers as a result of offshoring in either country.

2008 also saw the initial discussions to form The British Philippine Outsourcing Council (BPOC) in London with a number of key industry players coming together to try to replicate the success that BPAP had experienced in The United States.

Nearshore to Offshore

Some of the other English speaking markets have themselves been traditional nearshore options for their larger neighbours. Canada had boomed as an outsourcing destination for US call centre traffic but the popularity of The Philippines coupled with an appreciating Canadian dollar has meant that some call centre traffic has now been offshored to The Philippines although on a far smaller scale than American business. Ireland too has found its popularity reducing based in part due to the strength of the Euro currency. Ireland's own offshore market had traditionally been based on a mult-lingual offering due to its strong language skills. Much of the work offshored from Ireland to The Philippines has been part of deals done involving British based call traffic but there are a few Irish companies outsourcing to Manila on their own behalf. Of course, Ireland itself is a relatively small market with only 4 million people so the numbers of Filipino agents serving its marketplace has been very small. The same is true of New Zealand where it continues to have a relatively small industry servicing the entire Australasian market. There are now a number of Filipino call centres servicing the New Zealand marketplace but far less than its larger neighbour.

Non-English Languages

Relatively few Filipinos study other European besides English which has hindered growth on the European continent. The majority of Filipinos who speak other European languages do so primarily for one of two reasons; the first group is people who are of mixed-race with one parent being Filipino and the other (typically although not exclusively the father) being of European descent. There are small pockets of Spanish, German, Italian, French and other nationalities living in The Philippines with their children. These children can often be reasonably fluent in these languages and may have spent some time living in these countries. There is also a second group of Filipinos who are described as Overseas Foreign Workers (OFWs). The majority of OFWs work in The Middle East or other parts of Asia such as Hong Kong, South Korea or Japan but there are large numbers in some European countries. OFWs are typically nurses or care assistants and there are a large number of domestic workers and non-skilled employees. Many of these OFWs lack the educational background to work in call centres but there is evidence that some of them (especially those with language skills) are finding employment in the sector on their return to The Philippines. The demand for non-English European languages outstrips supply and agents with these skills can expect a premium for these skills. There is evidence that this premium can be up to as much as 100% in certain circumstances. This can mean that call centre resources who speak languages such as German, French and Italian can be as expensive as countries in Eastern Europe such as Romania where there is a far more plentiful supply of call centre agents with these language skills. Despite all this, there are some call centres that not only conduct work in other European languages but also do it very well.

There is also demand for call centre services from other high-cost Asian countries such as Korea & Japan but the supply of these languages is very limited. There are a number of small scale successes with these languages but these account for a very small amount of the overall call centre market in The Philippines. India, Indonesia & Malaysia all have their own sizeable domestic call centre industries and the cost of agents there is low enough to not justify offshoring. China also has its own large domestic call centre industry but there have been a handful of cases where Chinese-language calls have been conducted in The Philippines normally as an add-on to English speaking calls. There are an estimated 1.5 million Chinese Filipinos and many of these will speak Chinese languages at home. However, the Chinese community is traditionally highly entrepreneurial in The Philippines and whilst many of the more wealthy of this community own call centre outsourcing companies in the country, very few of them choose to work in the industry. It is widely accepted that despite their small numbers, Chinese Filipinos own more than half of The Philippine economy.

Chapter 11

Legal & Political Framework

"Within Asia, The Philippine Government is second to none in the support and financial incentives it has offered to the call centre industry and this has been key in its growth. Negative perceptions remain but most foreign call centre companies believe these are unfair and do not reflect the present day situation".

For many decades, there has been widespread international criticism of the Philippine Government in areas such as Government effectiveness, the legal framework and corruption perception. There is also broad support that The Philippines is generally on par in these areas with other developing nations and the situation has seen steady but solid progress in these areas. Having spoken with many industry executives, I hear little but praise for The Philippine Government support for outsourcing. The fact that so many international outsourcing companies have invested so heavily in the country is a testament that the negative perceptions do not necessarily match the experiences of outsourcing executives. However, no book on conducting international business in The Philippines would be complete with addressing these issues and focusing on the way in which outsourcing companies deal with them.

Corruption Perception

Transparency International produces an annual perceptions index of the most corrupt countries in the world. In the 2012 report, The Philippines was ranked as the joint 105th most corrupt country alongside Mexico out of a total of 174 countries. The difficulty with the perceptions index is that negative perceptions take a long time to shake off and The Philippines still suffers from the negativity relating to the Marcos administration.

The current President, Benigno Aquino, has made the fight against corruption a key focus of his administration and there is plenty of belief that he is doing just that. A survey in October 2011 showed that 72% of the country believed he was capable of solving the corruption problem. Like most keen observers of Philippine politics, I firmly believe in his sincerity and ability to make huge improvements in this fight. Let's not forget that his parents, Ninoy Aquino & Cory Aquino (President from 1986 to 1992) both dedicated their lives to restoring democracy in the country and so he has a lot to live up to.

Benigno's predecessor was Gloria Arroyo who was President from 2001 to 2010 and she was constantly accused of corruption and electoral sabotage. However, despite these negative sentiments, her administration saw the rapid rise in the country's outsourcing sector especially in call centres. If corruption was as widespread in her administration as her detractors state, then the call centre industry doesn't seem to be effected. In fact, the very nature of the offshore call centre industry means that it's not vulnerable to corruption. Most companies are liable for little or no corporation tax and revenues are not coming from the Philippine market. The industry is not competing for Philippine Government work and there are no physical exports which could be prone to exploitation from corrupt officials. Having spoken with many leading industry executives, nobody has ever mentioned corruption as a reason not to invest in The Philippines. Overall, the outsourcing industry wants the Government to be stable and if corruption does exist as many believe, the industry does not appear to be concerned.

Most contractual agreements between outsourced suppliers and their clients are produced under the laws of the client's location. For example, a Texas-based client outsourcing to a Philippines entity will produce a contract under the laws of Texas. International outsourcing companies with a registered office in the same country as the client will typically be the signatory to the contract. Many of the Indian vendors with a Philippines operation will sign the agreement from their Indian entity or a US-subsidiary if one exists. Therefore, the courts in The Philippines do not need to be involved in contractual disputes between a vendor and their clients and so even if judges in The Philippines can be influenced, this has no bearing on a company's desire to outsource to a call centre in The Philippines. Of course, a vendor who leases a building in The Philippines from a Philippine entity is still subject to the laws of The Philippines but there have no reported cases of international companies expressing a concern over corruption in any disputes.

Data and Intellectual Property Security and Privacy

Many in the outsourcing industry were concerned that The Philippines had been slow in creating specific laws to deal with data privacy to bolster the reputation of the outsourcing sector. There have been a number of high-profile incidents where consumer data has been misappropriated from offshore call centres and although almost all of these were in India, the offshore sector as a whole has been tarnished by them.

In August 2012, The Philippine Government adopted the Data Privacy Act of 2012 ('Act') which is the first ever consolidated data privacy legislation in the country. The Act was based on Directive 95/46/EC of the European Union and the Asia Pacific Economic Cooperation ('APEC') Information Privacy Framework and is considered to be one of the strongest pieces of related legislation in the world. The call industry was instrumental in supporting this legislation and believes it will strengthen the reputation of the country in an area where many foreign investors felt the country was weak. The only criticism of the bill I have encountered is how well it will be enforced in the courts. It has yet to be tested so only time will tell how effective it is in practice.

Labour Laws

Within The Philippines, employees are given a large amount of rights under The Labor Code of The Philippines. Some industry executives have stated that they believe that the country's labour laws are more inflexible than those in other offshore destinations such as India. It's more difficult to terminate non-performing employees in The Philippines than in India and the costs associated with termination can be high. Although some changes have been made such as changes to section 130 of the Labor Code which used to prohibit females from working between 10pm and 6am, some industry executives suggest that the laws need an overhaul.

In the Philippines, a dismissed employee has the right to question the validity of his dismissal. Once questioned before the proper labor authorities, the employer has the burden of establishing the validity of the dismissal by proving that the dismissal was for just and/or authorized cause and that the dismissal was done after the employer had complied with procedural due process

The Trade Union Congress of The Philippines and outsourcing industry representatives signed an agreement in April 2013 signaling the launch of the "BPO Workers Association of the Philippines", which aims to protect and improve productivity among industry workers. Although there is some discontent with the forming of such a union, it is widely considered that it strikes a fair balance between protecting the working rights of Filipinos and ensuring a flexible labour force.

Instability

Another area where the country has had a poor reputation is in terms of political instability. The Fund for Peace produces a report which ranks countries on their likelihood to become a failed state. The obvious contenders such as Somalia, Afghanistan and Sudan are always close to the top in their reports and The Philippines should not be considered alongside these countries. The Philippines has slowly been improving and is now considered to be the 56th most unstable country in the world. Over the past 30 years, there have been a number of political coups. The two successful and most famous coups are both known as People Power Revolutions. The first was in 1986 and overthrew the Government of Ferdinand Marcos who was replaced by Corazon Aquino. The Aquino administration was the subject of a number of attempted coups but she remained in power until 1992.

In 2001, an impeachment trial of the then President Joseph "Erap" Estrada failed in The Senate and this heralded a 2nd people power revolution which saw him deposed as leader by Gloria Arroyo. Under her administration, there were several small-scale coup attempts which all failed. Since then, the country has experienced a period of economic prosperity which history has shown us generally coincide with periods of political stability. Continued economic growth in The Philippines is likely to further improve the perception of The Philippines in this area. The commonly head view among both Filipinos and the expats living in The Philippines is that the country is far more stable than international observers and the media give credit for. In fact, the perception of The Philippines as a whole is blighted by an insurgency in the south of the country where kidnappings are commonplace. This deflects from Metro Manila and the greater Luzon area where political instability is no more of an issue than in any developing country. Most importantly, the perception of instability has not deterred international outsourcing firms or their clients. The Philippines is now so entrenched as a call centre destination that it would take a significant and sustained period of instability to derail that and there is not even the remotest sign that this will happen.

Government Effectiveness

The World Bank produce a "Government Effectiveness Indicator" and The Philippines is currently ranked 51st out of 207 countries having made significant improvements in this area. The potential of the industry for job creation was considered so important by the administration of Gloria Arroyo that she and her team placed a great deal of focus on providing support to the industry. Their support includes a range of financial incentives, marketing support, assisted visits and support in the creation of The Business Processing Association of The Philippines (BPAP). The Government has also been open to lobbying by industry representatives to ensure a flexible legal framework for outsourcing companies to operate within.

Whilst some foreign investors may still have concerns over the effectiveness of The Philippine Government, few can doubt the impact that their incentives schemes have achieved. The country has 2 main incentive regimes administered under The Board of Investments (BOI) and The Philippines Economic Zone Authority (PEZA) and for both of these schemes; call centres are able to receive very good incentives. The BOI incentives provide for tax holidays, the employment of foreign nationals and certain tax credits. The PEZA scheme allows for some additional incentives but the call centre must be based in a PEZA IT Zone or a PEZA building. Most importantly, both schemes offer far better incentives than India and many industry insiders believe that this is a key reason behind the growth of the industry in The Philippines. I have omitted from providing the full details of The BOI & PEZA schemes as I fully expect the incentives to be amended in the near to mid-term. The Philippines has now established itself as a strong player in this field and The Government must come out with revised plans which maximise tax receipts from the industry without deterring foreign investors from such a large job-creating industry.

Chapter 12

The Social Impact

"Lower birth rates, an increase in sexually transmitted diseases & employees seeing less of their families have all been blamed on the outsourcing boom in The Philippines but there is little doubt that is has also contributed to improving living standards".

Since the offshoring boom started in The Philippines at the start of the millennium, the social impact of the call centre industry has been little short of phenomenal. Its impact is felt far beyond the call centre agents to all levels of Philippine society from the wealthy conglomerates who build the buildings through to the siblings of call centre workers whose college fees are being paid for off the back of the outsourcing boom.

Improvements in living standards

The economy has taken a massive boost from the billions of dollars which now flow into the country ever year. This has created a large numbers of jobs in other sectors supporting the call centres including in security, catering, construction, telecommunications, technology and elsewhere. Unofficial estimates suggest that over 1 million indirect jobs have been created as a result of the call centre industry. The salaries of the call centre agents are well above the national average and this money is feeding through across the spectrum. Although many outsourcing companies have been enjoying tax holidays as incentives to invest, the employees have been paying tax which has fuelled the Government coffers and this has been much needed. GDP per capita is still languishing behind most of Asia but things are definitely on the rise. The demand for staff from the call centre industry is also changing employment practices in the non-call centre industry. For example, the minimum salary for a public school teacher is 17,255 pesos per month and for a nurse is 18,549 pesos. A team-leader in a call centre will earn far more than that and so other industries are having to increase their own salaries to compete. Overall, the figures for The Philippine economy are very strong. The stock index is at an all-time having increased nearly 200% in 3 years. Inflation is relatively low and this is being helped by a strong currency which is being fuelled by foreign currency flows from the outsourcing industry. The Philippine economy grew by 7.3% in 2010, the fastest since democracy was restored to the country in 1986.

The 24/7 culture

One major impact of the call centre industry on society undoubtedly comes from the hours which most agents work. The majority of the agents work night shifts and this, in itself, has created a culture change. Although, it was rarely enforced, it was actually illegal to employ females to work night shift in The Philippines when the call centre industry started. The controversial "section 130" of The Philippines Labor code prohibited work for females between 10pm and 6am but this wasn't that unusual given that hardly anyone worked night-shifts. The rules have now been changed but these "unsociable" hours mean that call centre agents spend less time with their family which is so fundamental to Philippine society. However, before the call centre industry, the major opportunities for young Filipinos came in the form of working abroad in areas such as The Middle East, North America or in the more prosperous countries of Asia. Most parents believe that the inconvenience of their children working night-shifts is a far better alternative than only seeing them once a year on their return from Saudi Arabia. I've recently spoken with a Filipino friend of mine who says there is evidence that the call centre industry could even be reducing the birth rate in The Philippines! The country has always had one of the highest birth rates in Asia and far higher than in The West but it has dropped significantly over the past 10 years. Although the evidence is anecdotal, I have little doubt that the unsociable hours and lifestyle are at least having some impact. Some might argue that the slowing down of the high birth rate might actually be good the country as a whole as even with this slowdown, the country's population is still growing rapidly. Manila is now very much a 24-hour society as anything from transport to shops, bars and restaurants serve the needs of call centre workers and this is all happening in a country where all the Filipino-language television stations still close down throughout the night.

The Provincial Impact

With all of this, the real impact of the call centre industry is even starker in the provinces outside of Metro Manila where incomes are substantially lower. The call centre industry is one factor increasing urbanisation in the capital which is already the most densely populated city on the planet. The economies of the smaller cities are massively different to the metropolis of Manila. Many of the brightest of graduates in smaller cities tend to move away to Manila or abroad to seek employment opportunities. Even small call centres in these cities have helped to reverse this trend and just like in Manila are creating support industries for local entrepreneurs although on a much smaller scale. The trickle-down effect of these new call centre jobs will help to revolutionise these cities. The fact that these centres are often locally-owned will also offer wealth-creating opportunities for locals rather than simply funding the coffers of foreign-based outsourcing vendors.

The future

Whilst the current situation is generally positive for The Philippines, there are potential risks to the society from the scale of the industry such as the following:

- What happens to the 20-something's when they're 30-somethings? Will they still want to work night shifts in call centres? Will there be other industries that can use the skills they've acquired or will they simply move abroad as previous generations have done.
- What happens if there is a slow-down in call centre traffic? Lets' not forget that companies have tended to offshore the more basic interactions which could be at risk from automation. A slow-down could reverse the positive trends we've seen.
- Is the large number of night-shifts going to have any long-term impact on the health of the employees? There is evidence to suggest it could without preventative measures.

The lives of many Filipinos have been positively influenced by the growth of the call centre industry. However, you don't create an industry of half a million people and generating billions of pounds in a developing nation without having a major impact. Population growth in The Philippines over the last 12 years is nearly twice that of The United States. These additional 17 million people are going to need jobs at some point and they're going to have to come from somewhere.

Chapter 13

The Philippines and Its Competition

"The Philippine call centre industry does not exist in isolation. It's difficult to think of a developing nation where English is widely spoken which would not be ecstatic to take call centre jobs away from The Philippines"

The volume of jobs call centre jobs created in both India & The Philippines has attracted the attention of developing nations around the world with everyone wanting a piece of the call centre pie. The more people I speak with about various locations, the more different views I receive. However, there are a number of nations whose call centre industry poses a threat to growth in The Philippines and below are some of the more common ones:

South Africa

There is a sizeable call centre industry in South Africa and the Government there has offered financial incentives which are even more advantageous than those offered by The Philippines. However, I am often baffled by the reasons why very few international outsourcing companies have entered the South African marketplace and why those who have established themselves there have failed to expand on anywhere near the scale achieved in The Philippines. In fact, Teletech were very vocal about their decision to enter the market but then left the country having failed to achieve any success. They set up a call centre in Cape Town in 2007 with the intention of creating 3,500 jobs in the country by 2012. In 2010, they left the country and sold their premises to a local business. Company insiders inform me that they struggled to sell South Africa as a destination to potential clients as it had a higher cost base than their other offshore locations without offering any additional benefits. There are several large call centres still in South Africa including CCI, Aegis & Teleperformance who operate alongside a number of locally owned vendors. The country's industry is far more skewed to The UK than the US marketplace due to historical links and a similar time zone. Most industry analysts expect to see reasonable growth in the South African marketplace but it does not have the same potential for scale as The Philippines and its cost base is higher with premium vendors charging in the region of $17-$21 per agent hour.

Egypt

Whilst The Arab Spring of 2011 is widely viewed as a positive step for Egyptian democracy, its outsourcing industry has suffered as a result of the instability. Egypt had tried to position itself as a global player in the broader BPO space offering services in English, Arabic and a range of European languages. In The UK, The Egyptians spent vast amounts of money including once having the largest stand at the country's premier call centre event known as Call Centre Expo which at the time was held in Birmingham's National Exhibition Centre. The country's success was limited but did become the home for a major call centre for international mobile phone operator Vodafone where they took calls from countries such as The UK and Australia. During the uprising, much of the country's telecommunications and internet networks failed to operate effectively & Vodafone were left in the embarrassing situation of having to quickly reroute calls to other countries. The power vacuum left after the uprising has led many companies to adopt a wait and see approach to Egypt and it's no longer considered a major threat to The Philippines industry. Cairo's decline as an outsourcing destination was highlighted in a report by Tholons which reduced its ranking from the 49th most suitable destination for outsourcing down to 58th. Future prosperity in Egypt relies heavily on political stability and until this is in place, it's difficult to see it challenging The Philippines.

India

It's hard to talk about the competition for The Philippines call centre industry without talking about the old rival of India whose industry seemed unassailable before the rise of The Philippines. Many centres there have now reduced in size dramatically or even closed purely as a result of the success of The Philippines. Many Indian outsourcing companies seem resigned to defeat in the global call centre race and there is now an increasing focus within India on other forms of outsourcing. However, it's not unthinkable for India to rise again and retake its position as the global leader in call centres. The technical education in India is far superior to that of The Philippines and it's hard to see The Philippines becoming the global leader in technical support. As the volume of contact centre interactions switch to non-voice activities, India will continue to see itself as a strong player. Also, many of the world's leading call centre and BPO companies are now Indian-owned and they all still bullish about India's future potential. Many companies still choose India for their call centre operations and the country's huge English-speaking and highly technically-savvy population are very popular with a number of international companies. Like The Philippines, India's capacity for scale is also considered a major positive point with many global companies. India will continue to outperform The Philippines in some other types of outsourcing services.

Jamaica

Many countries in The Caribbean have call centre industries including Jamaica. The legacy of British rule means that English is widely spoken and is the only official language. A number of international players have entered the market on a relatively small scale and there is a widely accepted view that the industry will grow there. Its relative proximity to The United States makes it easier for American companies to manage their outsource providers.

The Dominican Republic

The Dominican Republic has the advantage over The Philippines in that it can offer bi-lingual English and Spanish resources. It has a booming call centre industry but its population of around 10 million means that its industry will never have the scale of The Philippines. Due to its proximity to The United States, it pitches itself as a low-cost nearshore destination and many companies include The Dominican Republic on their shortlist of possible locations.

Pakistan

Pakistan continues to be very envious of India's rise in the outsourcing world. The industry within Pakistan is significant but dwarfs in comparison to that of The Philippines or even its neighbours in India. The political instability in Pakistan is one of the main reasons that global outsourcing companies have stayed out of Pakistan and there is no signs that this will change anytime soon. However, a number of companies do outsource call centre work to Pakistan and many believe that its industry will grow but not at a rate that will eat into the dominance of The Philippines.

Eastern Europe

The main advantages for Eastern European centres are the large availability of European language resources. Costs in Eastern Europe are higher than The Philippines but many like the fact that many of these countries are now part of The European Union making data protection and intellectual properties more strongly regulated. Common locations for call centre activity in Eastern Europe include Poland & Romania. Their proximity to the major economies of Europe is viewed positively by many companies located there.

Ireland

The Irish call centre industry boomed in the 1990's in no small part due to American technology companies entering the market. These centres were established to provide call centre services to The UK, Continental Europe and to a lesser extent, The United States. The appreciation of The Euro means that it has become less popular for large scale projects. However, Ireland is still seen a high-end call centre location due to its highly talented workforce.

Domestic centres

There is no doubt that domestic outsourcers in The USA, UK and Australia have all upped their game since the explosion in offshoring. There were many who predicted that the onshore operations in high-cost countries would have been all but gone by now but this hasn't happened and many of them are prospering. A number of high-profile companies have been very public about their decisions to bring call centre jobs back onshore despite the associated increase in costs and these were all positively viewed by both the media and general public. The economic downturn in The United States & United Kingdom has softened the labour market which means call centres located there have been able to attract good talent with minimal wage inflation. Home based call centre agents are also on the increase in Western countries which offer reduced costs over traditional office based environments. Many companies have now made up their minds whether they offshore or not and those who do generally have clear strategies as to what work is best kept onshore and what can be moved to lower cost base locations.

Conclusion

There is no shortage of competition for The Philippines. Some offer very similar value propositions to The Philippines bit it's hard to see any of them taking considerable market share. As clients of outsourcing companies become increasingly comfortable with multi-shoring, it's inevitable some of these countries will take business which could otherwise have been placed in The Philippines. Of all the offshore locations, only India is anywhere near the size of The Philippines. Like India, The Philippines has proven that it can handle call centre projects on a massive scale which isn't the case in the other locations. The Philippines does not need to look over its shoulder at what other offshore locations are doing. It is the market leader and if it continues to focus on ensuring vast quantities of quality call centre agents, it will continue to succeed. Some countries may look to provide short-term financial incentives to build their market share. This has been tried in South Africa with limited success but others may also consider this. Many people believe that The Philippines will look to maximise the tax revenues from the call centre and other outsourcing industry by reducing the financial incentives it offers. The country needs to ensure that this does not make it uncompetitive compared with other locations.

Chapter 14

The Future

"Our position in the industry is not a God-given right. We have to work hard as an industry" – Karen Batungbacal de Venecia, Senior Country Operations Officer, JP Morgan Chase

Whilst I was very confident of my prediction in 2002 about The Philippines being the home of more call centre agents than India, the future now that the country has achieved this is far harder to predict. There are a number of challenges and opportunities both internally and externally which have the power to shape the future size and structure of the industry.

Internally, the industry faces 2 challenges; the availability of large volumes of quality personnel and price competitiveness. The major factors influencing price competitiveness are inflation and the value of the Philippines peso. To date, inflation in areas such as the cost of office space and wages has been offset by lower telecommunications costs, economies of scale and shrinking margins. With the total Philippine economy growing rapidly, some inflation is inevitable and so costs to clients will have to rise. The rising value of the peso is also a concern for outsourcing companies and some are starting to ask at whether there is a tipping point in its value where offshoring to The Philippines is no longer viable. We are a long way from that tipping point but the combination of inflation and an increasing currency could start to make clients and vendors look at alternative locations. Of course, The Philippines hopes that those alternative locations will be the next wave cities and even other locations within the country. The availability of suitable employees also has to be considered if the industry is to grow at current rates. The initiatives undertaken by Government & private companies to bolster the labour supply have had an impact but the scale of the industry means a colossal effort is required to meet supply. The shift outside of Metro Manila will assist with this but this alone will not solve the problem.

Perhaps the biggest threat to The Philippines comes from its own success. If other forms of outsourcing grow rapidly in the country offering higher salaries and dayshift working, this could eat into the limited availability of suitable talent as happened in India. Analysts say that by 2016, call centres will for the first time constitute less than 50% of all outsourcing revenue in The Philippines. From a country perspective, this is good news as it cannot rely so much on one industry but from a call centre perspective, this poses even greater challenges.

Externally, the country faces challenges from a wide range of other countries and also from the ever changing landscape of the call centre outsourcing industry as a whole. The industry I joined over 20 years barely resembles the industry which exists today and the next decade will see even greater changes. Many of the human interactions which happen today will be replaced by self-service technologies and the fact that it is often the more basic interaction types which are offshored poses a genuine threat. Consumers are becoming increasingly demanding and the interactions which are not handled by self-service will become increasingly complex and call centre agents will increasingly need technical expertise and critical thinking skills. As the balance of economic power switches from West to East, The Philippines also needs to consider new markets for its services and this means a greater focus on the teaching of other languages besides English.

Outsourcing is moving away from focusing on cost arbitrage towards total business transformation and for many Philippine vendors, this is an alien concept. Philippine vendors need to improve the way in which they assist the business of their clients and not simply be a low cost resource. Most of this strategic thinking is still done outside of The Philippines in North America, Europe, Australia & now in India and this has to change if Philippine vendors are to move up the value chain.

Another factor which could impact outsourcing is the rise of captive centres within The Philippines. The Philippines is no longer considered a risky option for foreign call centre traffic and so companies could be more inclined to go it alone without an outsourced partner. Many of the larger operations being established now are captive facilities and whilst this is good for the country, it is not necessarily good news for outsourced vendors.

The Opportunities

The ways in which businesses service their customers is going through a period of change. The telephone will remain the single most important communication channel but we're starting to see an increasing number of companies view social media interaction as one way forward. Web chat and email support have both been around for some time and growth in these areas is far slower than was predicted but they are on the rise. Many companies are adopting a "call reduction strategy" where they attempt to shift as many interactions away from the telephone and towards cheaper options. The Philippines will undoubtedly be one of the beneficiaries of this.

The Philippines remains a popular destination for call centre traffic with clients and there is no sign of this changing but the country and its industry must pre-empt the changing climate and respond accordingly. The relative ease with which half a million call centre jobs have moved to The Philippines is viewed positively within the country but it should also be a seen as a warning sign.

About the author

My name is Rob O'Malley and I have worked in the call centre outsourcing industry for over 20 years. I started my career with Merit Direct (now SITEL) before joining Teleperformance. In 2000, I moved to The Philippines where I worked as a consultant for a company who were setting up as an outsourced vendor. Although I'd only planned to be in Manila for 6 months, I ended up working in the call centre industry there for 6 years. Since returning to the live in The UK in 2006, I have continued to work as a consultant to UK businesses looking to establish or improve their outsourcing in The Philippines. In 2009, I was elected as Chairman to the newly formed British Philippine Outsourcing Council (BPOC) and I've held this position to this day. On my regular trips back to the country, I'm often dumbfounded by not only the way in which the industry has changed but also the way in which the industry has been able to change a country of over 100 million people.

www.ingramcontent.com/pod-product-compliance
Lightning Source LLC
Chambersburg PA
CBHW051333170526
45166CB00002B/794